Ultimate Freedom

Ultimate Freedom

Beyond Free Will

KEITH LEHRER

OXFORD
UNIVERSITY PRESS

Oxford University Press is a department of the University of Oxford. It furthers the University's objective of excellence in research, scholarship, and education by publishing worldwide. Oxford is a registered trade mark of Oxford University Press in the UK and certain other countries.

Published in the United States of America by Oxford University Press
198 Madison Avenue, New York, NY 10016, United States of America.

© Oxford University Press 2024

All rights reserved. No part of this publication may be reproduced, stored in a retrieval system, or transmitted, in any form or by any means, without the prior permission in writing of Oxford University Press, or as expressly permitted by law, by license, or under terms agreed with the appropriate reproduction rights organization. Inquiries concerning reproduction outside the scope of the above should be sent to the Rights Department, Oxford University Press, at the address above.

You must not circulate this work in any other form
and you must impose this same condition on any acquirer.

Library of Congress Cataloging-in-Publication Data
Names: Lehrer, Keith, author.
Title: Ultimate freedom / by Keith Lehrer.
Description: New York, NY, United States of America : Oxford University Press, [2024] |
Includes bibliographical references and index. |
Identifiers: LCCN 2023011395 (print) | LCCN 2023011396 (ebook) |
ISBN 9780197695029 (hardback) | ISBN 9780197695043 | ISBN 9780197695050 |
ISBN 9780197695036 (epub)
Subjects: LCSH: Self. | Will. | Choice.
Classification: LCC BF697 .L367 2024 (print) | LCC BF697 (ebook) |
DDC 155.2—dc23/eng/20230720
LC record available at https://lccn.loc.gov/2023011395
LC ebook record available at https://lccn.loc.gov/2023011396

DOI: 10.1093/oso/9780197695029.001.0001

Printed by Integrated Books International, United States of America

I dedicate this book to my four granddaughters with love.
They have more greatly enriched my life than they can imagine.
Clara Lehrer
Elsa Lehrer
Sydney Lehrer
Harper Lehrer

Contents

Acknowledgments — ix

Introduction: Freedom of Choice and Acceptance — 1

1. Preference, Reason, and Agency — 9
2. Freedom of Choice: Source and Leeway — 29
3. Reason, Preference, and Freedom — 47
4. Determinism, Ultimate Preference, and the Consistency Claim — 76
5. Freedom of Choice and Conflict Resolution — 106
6. Freedom, Representation, and Consciousness — 127

Epilogue: Freedom and Two Systems — 142

Appendix: On Keith Lehrer's Conception of a Power Preference — 149
Bibliography — 153
Index — 161

Acknowledgments

Most of the material in these chapters is newly written, though I make use of ideas and arguments from my previously published work cited in the bibliography, especially that which has been published in the *Journal of Ethics*. The one exception is Chapter 3, which is full revision of "Reason and Autonomy," *Social Philosophy and Policy* 20 (2) (2003): 177–198. © 2003 Social Philosophy and Policy Foundation, published by Cambridge University Press. It is republished with the permission of the Foundation. There is a reproduction in black and white of an image in the public domain, Claude Monet (1873) *Sheltered Path*, Philadelphia Museum of Art. Gift of Mr. and Mrs. Hughs Norment in honor of William H. Donner, 1972, 1972-227-1.

I wish to express my gratitude to Carl Wagner, who provided a mathematical proof of a claim I made about conflict resolution and a fixed-point theorem that occurs as an appendix. It is an application of work he did in an earlier collaboration of ours that has been ongoing and is a special accomplishment in which I take great pride.

I am especially indebted to Joseph Keim Campbell for provoking my current effort by his critical development of my work. Without his support the current manuscript would not have been written. Of comparable importance to the project was my colleague Michael McKenna, who helped revise my earlier efforts. I am deeply indebted to him for the stimulation of his brilliant conversation at the Arizona Inn, as well as for his more specific discussion of my work and his crediting me with a central argument concerning the *consequence argument* in his essay cited. Then there is Angelo

Corlett, who read and commented on an earlier version of the text in great detail as well as writing about my work and encouraging me to publish in the *Journal of Ethics* over the years on the topic of freedom, which kept me in touch with some leading literature. I thank him for all his dedication to my philosophical work but especially for his deep friendship. Mylan Engel is a primary cause of my continued labors, as he arranged a conference, "Keith and Me," for discussion of my previous work, and another, "Keith and Me 2," provoked by the manuscript of the current work. His comments and editorial assistance were invaluable. The thought and discussion of participants in these conferences was remarkable philosophy. I thank them all. I am also grateful to Cathleen Johnson for her very generous efforts and financial support of the Center for Philosophy of Freedom in organizing "Keith and Me 2."

There are others to whom I am indebted in various ways, especially Josh Cangelosi, a graduate student who arranged workshop discussions of my work. Another graduate student, Phoebe Chan, met with me often informally for invaluable philosophical discussion and suggestions, as did Agrawal Ritwik. They offered their time and formidable insight without formal credit. A friend, Gerald Swatez, provided weekly stimulation of issues related to philosophy of mind that influenced the manuscript. I am grateful to all of these people for their assistance and philosophical insights.

There are others to whom I wish to express my gratitude, especially David Schmidtz and Cathleen Johnson for financial as well as personal support of the "Keith and Me" conferences. My thanks to my talented and loving wife, Adrienne Lehrer, who assisted me with proofreading, style, and form. She is always invaluable. My thanks to Dylan Kern and Phoebe Chan for work on the bibliography.

I also wish to express my gratitude to Peter Ohlin of Oxford University Press for his guidance and advice leading to publication with the press, and Brent Matheny for his splendid and diligent production efforts, especially with obtaining permissions for reproduction of images. Finally, I wish to thank Otavio Bueno for offering publication of the discussions of this book in the Synthese Library in a book edited by Mylan Engel and Joseph Keim Campbell. My deepest gratitude to all who have devoted their efforts to my philosophy.

Ultimate Freedom

Introduction

Freedom of Choice and Acceptance

The purpose of this introduction is to explain the conception of freedom I wish to defend and the connection of it to a conception of determinism. What I say here should not be taken as a refined formulation of doctrine or argument in defense. It is a succinct guide to what I shall refine and argue. I insist on this because a brief formulation of doctrine and argument may become the focus of critical discussion. Critical discussion is always welcome, but my fully articulated view is deep within the chapters that follow rather than in this brief rendition of what is to follow.

My Philosophical Method

My method is motivated by a deep-seated conviction about human nature and intellectual capacity. I am impressed and motivated by a human capacity to reconfigure how we conceive our world, ourselves in our world, and, even most remarkably perhaps, our world in us conceived by us. I seek a theory to explain the exercise of that capacity in terms of reflective freedom of choice in practice and theory. My goal is to explain as much as possible and to leave as little unexplained about freedom of choice as I must. I do not claim to refute all conflicting theories, though I acknowledge disagreement with the most salient opposition. I seek to maximize explanation, not refutation. I hope to convince you that I have explained the cogency and power of freedom of choice in practical pursuits and intellectual inquiry. That quest motivates this essay.

The theory I am about to unfold is a general theory of freedom of choice consistently combining preference and choice with scientific explanation. It is not intended as a semantic analysis of the ordinary use of the terms "freedom" and "choice." It is an attempt to create a conception of freedom to explain the most important choices we make rather than to analyze ordinary use of words. The theory of freedom of choice is based on a higher-order evaluation of our thought and language to produce a reconfiguration that reveals one form of choice that makes us special in the scientific order of things. My method is top down rather than bottom up. It is an attempt to distinguish our intellectual powers of choice from the animals with whom we share many physical capacities. In theory of knowledge Sosa (1991) defended a distinction between animal knowledge and reflective knowledge. I later (2000) advanced a similar distinction between primitive knowledge and discursive or metaknowledge. The present work is based on a distinction in theory of choice between primitive or first-order response and reflective choice or metalevel choice. The distinction is a philosophical narrative invented to describe experience and behavior in a way that reveals the character of freedom of choice.

I am, however, influenced by scientific theories of human capacities, especially those of cognitive science and economics that capture a unique character of human choice. I have neglected a great deal of philosophical literature of great merit in my attempt to change how we think and describe ourselves as we exercise a uniquely human power of choice. If my theory of freedom of choice leaves you with the feeling and conviction that not much of what you do is an exercise of such freedom, you have understood my objective. Freedom of choice is a form of choice that transcends the quotidian. It is the exercise of a higher power of reasoning and reflection in defense of our reasons for preference that empowers us in choice. Most of the time we act without the exercise of this power of preference. Freedom of choice is the exercise of this power.

Free Will and Moral Responsibility

I begin noting that this essay is about freedom of choice. Freedom of choice is not entailed by free will conceived of as doing what one desires because freedom of choice is not guaranteed by doing what one desires. Doing what one willingly and wholeheartedly desires is often what is meant by free will in current discussion motivated by Frankfurt (1971, 1988). When desire is evaluated positively and one reflectively considers alternatives and prefers to satisfy it, then freedom of choice may be consistent with free will. But preference, not desire, is what is required for free choice, on my account. This is not an essay about desire-articulated free will!

Moreover, this is not just an essay about moral responsibility. Freedom of choice is logically independent of moral responsibility. Sometimes freedom of choice is based on moral reflection and concerns. Sometimes, to the contrary, freedom of choice is based on practical concerns that lie outside the moral domain. The current literature, resulting from Strawson (1962) and Frankfurt (1971), make the conception of free will dependent on moral responsibility. I have already noted that the conception of freedom of choice is not an account of free will, which supports the logical independence of freedom of choice from moral responsibility based on desire. But my claim of independence runs deeper. Free will skepticism is much discussed in connection with responsibility by Pereboom (2014), for example. But my observation about freedom of choice is compatible with moral skepticism. Even if one is a skeptic about morals, including moral responsibility, that would be logically consistent with an affirmation of freedom of choice. Suppose I am a moral skeptic. I still confront alternatives that lie before me in my life. Though I reject moral judgment, being a moral skeptic, I might be no skeptic about the importance to me of choices in my life. Those choices might lead me to deliberate about alternatives, about what option to choose among the alternatives. That I deliberate about alternatives that I believe are options does not entail that the options are genuine in the sense that whatever I choose I could have chosen otherwise. My point here is not about justification but about the logical connection between freedom of choice and moral responsibility. I can understand those philosophers, like Strawson, who argue that our reactive attitudes depend on the assumption of free will, and perhaps he is right that we connect moral judgments of responsibility with judgments and conversation about free will. Michael McKenna (2012) makes the case lucidly and convincingly for this connection illustrated in moral conversation. Some may even suppose the connection is entailment. But it is not. The connection depends on a moral principle, not a principle of logical entailment.

This failure of logical entailment may be illustrated by one committed to morals and moral principles. It is logically consistent in moral theory to attribute moral responsibility to a person who lacked freedom of choice for a deed, if one holds a moral principle attributing moral responsibility for the choice of a father to a son, and it is equally logically consistent to deny moral responsibility to an agent who exercises freedom of choice when placed in a moral situation compromised by a history of misery.

Returning to the moral skeptic, must a moral skeptic deny that he has freedom of choice? No. He or she still lives a life with choice. Moral skeptics may think some choices are free choices explained by their personal preferences among alternatives. Whether one thinks of choices as moral choices or rejects morals and thinks of them as simply practical choices, perhaps ones with costs and benefits amorally considered, freedom of choice confronts one. One committed to morals, to a life of moral responsibility, may argue that the commitment morally commits one to affirm free will or even freedom of choice. That is a moral commitment and an important one. But a moral skeptic who considers freedom of choice may with perfect consistency put her hand over her mouth in silence when asked what she has to say about the moral implications of her free choice. In the discussion that follows I focus, nonetheless, on some of examples of free choice in moral matters. My point is that connection of free choice with moral responsibility is a matter of moral principle.

Free Choice

This is an essay about freedom of choice. My primary claim is simple to formulate though complicated to defend. It is that there is form of free choice revealing preference that I call *ultimate preference*. This freedom of choice gives us the title of the book, *ultimate freedom*, because it is a form of freedom of choice explained by ultimate preference. The preference is so-called because it is the ultimate explanation for the freedom of choice. The explanation is ultimate because it stands alone as an adequate explanation and is self-explanatory. Ultimate preference for a choice may itself be explained. But the free choice is explained by the ultimate preference rather than by what explains the ultimate preference. The ultimate preference is sufficient as the explanation of the choice. I have called the ultimate preference a *power preference* because it may be a preference for higher-level preferences, if there are any, concerning the choice and because it is an active power exercised to form the preference for free choice.

Could Have Chosen Otherwise

The ultimate preference entailing free choice also entails that the agent could have chosen otherwise. Since the power preference is a power exercised in favor of a choice of a specified alternative, it is also a power that might have been exercised as an ultimate preference not to so choose. Free choice is explained by a power preference that is an ultimate preference. If the agent had preferred not to make that choice, an ultimate preference would have explained that instead. Whether choosing as the agent does or otherwise, the choice is within the power of the agent. It is a conception of free choice that requires an alternative to what is chosen. In the popular vernacular, the free choice is up to the agent. Such an agent has alternative possibilities or leeway of choice and action. This conception of free choice is philosophically controversial, and the extension of it to cover the popular notion of free will is even more so. I offer no apology. Innovation in philosophy is the mother of controversy.

Freedom and Determinism

The defense of ultimate preference and ultimate explanation will be elaborated in the chapters below. Since they raise questions about the consistency of the doctrine with accounts of the causality and determinism of choice, I will state my views in the matter briefly here and elaborate subsequently. This matter is sometimes formulated as the question of *compatibilism* of free choice with causality and determinism. I have been a party to this way of formulating the issue, which has provoked a classification of views into compatibilism and incompatibilism theories about freedom and determinism. Whatever the merits of the terminology introduced into the discussion at the time, the complications and sophistication of a variety of views of freedom and determinism subsequently introduced into the discussion render the classification ambiguous at this stage. The logical consistency of the views depends on what is meant by them, and there is no simple standard to the meaning of the terms describing freedom and determinism to which one can appeal in philosophical discussion, as Balaguer (2009) also notes.

I have briefly said what I shall mean by *free choice* and shall allow myself a brief if equally controversial account of determinism. My account of determinism is in terms of universal scientific principles. Scientific principles so conceived are universal generalizations, often called laws. Determinism requires that such laws cover all of nature, including, of course, human choice. I reject the view that such universal generalizations are modal principles or that they are laws that make things happen. Moreover, I reject the view that they always provide explanations of what is deduced from them about specific states or events. The principles of geometry allow us to deduce the length of a hypotenuse between two objects from the sides of a right triangle without explaining why the objects rest at that distance from each other. Similarly, deduction from the general principles of determinism is not always explanatory. Science may have the capacity to explain everything, indeed, everything may have a scientific explanation, but the deduction from the general principles of determinism is not always sufficient for such explanation. Moreover, as I shall argue, explanation is not generally transitive, though deduction from the principles of determinism is generally transitive. There is no automatic connection between determinism and scientific explanation.

Unification of Science and Agency

The preceding summary of my views on free choice and scientific determinism allows for a logically consistent unification of agency, free choice, and science. Free choice results from ultimate explanation provided by a power preference. But determinism does not entail an explanation of free choice. More crucially, given the failure of general transitivity of explanation, power preference may be the ultimate explanation, an adequate standalone explanation of free choice, given determinism. That allows, however, for the possibility of scientific explanation of every event including free choice, however it results from ultimate preference. We can, therefore, acknowledge the possibility of complete scientific explanation of everything, including free choice. However, determinism does not entail such complete explanation. Whether we have free choice depends on how choice is explained, by ultimate preference or in some other scientific manner. My account is a unification theory of agency and science. Is that *compatibilism*? We need a new definition of the term to cover the innovation proposed in the subsequent chapters, or we need to neglect this mode of classification.

Some new classification may be appropriate. The idea that freedom requires that when a person chooses a course of action, the person could have chosen another, has been called the leeway theory, implying that a free choice requires the leeway to choose an alternative. Another view is the sourcehood view which requires that the person must be the source of the choice. Both of these views are often described by the requirement that the choice is up to the agent. A traditional view is that the choice, often called a volition, must be caused by the agent. These various views are often taken as competing with each other. The proposal above requiring that a free choice results from the exercise of a power preference, which is an ultimate preference, satisfies all of these requirements of free choice. As an exercise of a power of the agent resulting in an ultimate preference, it is a preference caused by the agent. As an exercise of a power of preference, it would also be an ultimate preference for preferring to choose an alternative, or simply not choosing it. Finally, as an ultimate preference, a preference formed because of the self-explanatory preference for having that preference would be caused by the agent. Ultimate preference supplies an agent with leeway in choice that makes the agent the source and cause of the choice. The competitors blend into unification.

1
Preference, Reason, and Agency

In this monograph I am going to present a theory of freedom of choice, what I shall call *ultimate freedom*. Ultimate freedom might be called *reflective freedom* or alternatively, for special emphasis on rational defensibility of preference, *defensible freedom*. Ultimate freedom has two dimensions. The first is freedom of choice among alternatives or optionality. The theory is based on the role of higher-order preference in choice, reason, agency, and freedom. I have distinguished between first-order states like desire and belief that may arise in us unreflectively, leading directly to action, in contrast to higher-order states of preference and acceptance that are under the direction of reason and may guide us to reflective choice and decision.

There is a similarity in this to the distinction Daniel Kahneman (2011) insists on between the operations of system 1 and system 2 in choice. Kahneman gives us a list of features of how these systems operate, but the lack of the guidance of reason, especially statistical reason, in the operation of system 1 in action is contrasted with the ordered use of reason of system 2. I compare the contrast between first-order states and higher-order states. The higher-order states are states of reflection on representational content, including first-order states and their representational content. Kahneman thinks of system 1 as responding to impressions and feelings to produce rapid response. It is the fast system. System 2 involves a step-by-step process of reasoning. It directs attention to statistics and is by contrast slower and less efficient in response. It may be effective when considering and evaluating background information in an ordered and analytic mode. I shall follow Kahneman's terminology of system 1 and system 2, but I acknowledge a difference. Kahneman attributes belief to system 2, saying that system 1 operates with impressions and feeling rather than belief. This may only be terminological, but a standard view of inflexibility and fixation of belief leads me to attribute belief to first-order system. I contrast this with acceptance. I associate this with the optionality of accepting or rejecting what one and others believe in the light of ratiocination effected by system 2. The terminology of systems should not be read as ontology or even functional independence in either Kahneman or myself. The systems are simply modes of response that interact.

Suggesting a biological distinction to Kahneman's system 1 and system 2, McGilchrist (2009) draws a distinction between the R system and the L system. The R system is the system of the right brain, responding immediately from feeling and association without the intervention of ordered reasoning. The L system is the system of the left brain that engages in formal reasoning. The attribution of such functions to hemispheres of the brain is doubtful and may be ignored. What matters is the story of two interacting systems. These interacting systems are, therefore, modes of response in the formation of preference and direction of free choice. The suggestion of two interacting systems is explored by a number of philosophers, most notably Peter Railton (2014), whom I mention in connection Kahneman and McGilchrist because both suggest that the first-order system is the hero of the story, as do many philosophers. They do so because the system 1 mode of response is more attentive to the impressions of sense and the feelings connected with both sensory and interpersonal experience.

Note, for contrast to the idea of interacting systems, that Fodor (1983) drew a sharp functional contrast between an input system of modular representational responses that were automatic, encapsulated from background knowledge, and a central system that draws on background knowledge for reasoning. However,

Fodor's (1983) focus on the input system of modules also emphasizes the first-order system, though his distinction differs in an important way from the others. The output representations of an input system are, according to Fodor, transferred as input to a central system, but there is no transfer of central-system data to the encapsulated modules of the input system. It is an open question in the other theories whether and how the output of processing of the higher-order system may be transferred to the first-order system.

The emphasis on first-order response, whether system 1 in Kahneman, the input system in Fodor, or the R system in McGilchrist, should include an important feature of their own work and preference, namely, that their own scientific research is the product of a higher-order system of reflection. This is perhaps the most evident in Kahneman, whose work with Tversky revealed experimentally how system 1 leads to errors of judgment, particularly concerning probabilities, but also more generally. Indeed, it is fair to say that such experimentally established reservations were the basis of his scientific fame. I want, by contrast, perhaps connected with philosophical traditions favoring the role of reason, to write the story of the role of reason as the hero of the story of freedom of choice. Reason must have input from sensory experience, whether personal or interpersonal. Formal reasoning may lack feeling and sensory input. However, feelings and emotions are essential aspects of input and the direction of attention to it by the higher-order system and beyond that to the evaluation of higher-order patterns of reasoning. Nevertheless, the evaluation and judgment of reason, even abstract and formal features of reason, are essential to the proper function of freedom and agency in a way that makes reason the hero of the story. It guides the function of preference and acceptance in freedom of choice. Ultimate freedom is rational when defended in the higher-order system of reason, and that is what gives human agency the authority required for the defense of rational freedom of choice and action.

How Dare You!

I appreciate the role of experimental inquiry, and I value it, but it is important to consider what is clear and obvious in the natural course of human interaction as well. So, I begin with a line from the speech of a sixteen-year-old committed to the role of reason in human affairs, namely, Greta Thunberg. She addressed a group of influential adults in positions of power gathered to discuss climate change at the UN Summit on Climate Change and to consider what actions to take. She listened to their inadequate commitments to confront the problem. Some explicitly expressed the hope that the young might intervene to rescue us. Greta replied, "How dare you!" as she presented the scientific evidence, carefully packaged, of where the neglect of the problem of climate change would leave us. Her rhetoric implied a pair of simple truths. First, her audience had the ultimate free choice to act in a rational and reflective manner in response to the information about climate change. Second, they chose not to exercise that freedom. "How dare you!" There is no way that leaving this issue to an input module, to the R system, or to system 1 is going to explain why Greta is right, and the exercise of freedom and agency by her audience was not defensible.

There are many issues of this sort. Responding in ways that are comfortable to current feelings, beliefs, and social commitments, while refusing to follow the path of reason from scientific evidence to the acceptance of reasoned conclusions and the preference to choose to act on them, is not defensible by reason. There are so many other examples in which belief, what I attribute to the first-order system, is not rational or reflective. Consider the belief that you can prevent disastrous fires by just pouring water on fires without the need to burn away the accumulated fuel that feeds them. That has been the custom of forest management policy. The path of reason of the higher-order system leads to the scientific conclusion that the belief should be rejected. We rationally accept that it is essential to steadily burn away the accumulated fuel resulting from human intervention of fire suppression. We should prefer to burn away that accumulated fuel. But forest management experts, who know this, like those at the climate summit, fail to form the preferences to choose in accord with reason. The path of reason itself is not infallible. We are not infallible. We may sometimes fail to reach the truth. But reason is an engine that takes us deductively from truth to truth, or inductively, to the correct evaluation of the probability of truth. Reason, though it seems cold and abstract, makes preference and acceptance reasonable and leads us to defensible freedom of choice. Feelings of love and anger are not enough. You have to confront the discomfort of reason and truth to exercise ultimate freedom that is reflectively defensible.

Ultimate Freedom

So, what is ultimate freedom? I offer some sufficient conditions. The first is freedom of choice. Ultimate or defensible freedom may arise in ways beyond what I conceive of as sufficient, though the *capacity* to choose in the way I describe is necessary as well. If Greta were asked what would make the freedom of those she addresses defensible, she might tell my story. Where should we begin to articulate what is sufficient for ultimate and reflectively defensible freedom? I begin where I shall end, filling in elaboration and details as we consider alternatives. I distinguish belief and desire, which may arise in us rather unreflectively, from acceptance and preference, which are the responses of reason. There is some merit in having automatic responses available in many situations. What Patricia Churchland (1993) amusingly called the four "f's" of survival, feeding, fighting, fleeing, and reproduction, may be largely and frequently directed by belief and desire. But as we consider the broader issues of survival based on control of nuclear weapons and concern for climate change, we see the importance of using reason to guide what we accept and how we prefer to choose. Let me start with preference, distinguishing it from desire, because I consider it central in reflectively defensible freedom. The connection between freedom of choice and preference may seem obvious. The connection with reason is more controversial.

Preference and Optionality

The most important feature of preference for choice is that it entails a conception and conviction of options. When you prefer a choice of a course of action, you prefer it to something else. That is optionality. This is most obvious in the case of deliberation. If you deliberate about what to do, the outcome will reveal your preference for that alternative over others. Thomas Reid (1895) noted this, and I followed him (Lehrer 1960). Nelkin (2004), Kapitan (1986), and Cohen (2018) explored the implication of deliberation in detail. Reid originally argued that introspection of the activity of deliberation reveals the conviction of a choice of alternatives. Let us call the alternatives under deliberation a *profile*. Reflective freedom of choice reveals preference over a profile of alternatives. The person accepts that there was a profile including other alternatives, whatever the choice. This profile need not be elaborate. It involves minimally the alternative of not choosing the preferred alternative. If I deliberate about whether or not to go to my computer to work on my essay on freedom of choice, I accept that if I choose to do so, I had the alternative of choosing not to do it. This might involve consideration of some more detailed alternative, like going to my atelier to paint instead, something else I enjoy doing. But the alternative of not choosing to go to my computer confronts my preference and makes it a preference to choose. So preference and reflective freedom of choice involve acceptance of a profile of alternatives of choice, even if minimally, just choosing not to do as I actually choose.

Note that acceptance of a profile of alternatives does not entail that I actually can choose any other alternative, only that I accept that I can. However, the fact that I accept that I have alternatives, a profile of preferences, provides some justification for accepting the reality of alternatives. The acceptance of having a profile of alternatives, any one of which I can choose, is a condition of deliberation. Therefore, the acceptance of the alternatives has the status of being an essential ingredient of everyday practical existence, of common sense as it was described in the eighteenth century by Reid. Without such acceptance, deliberation would be a sham, reducing to consideration of what I *would* choose if I *had* a choice.

This position may seem controversial if you suppose that a person deliberating about what to do can actually choose among various alternatives. Some, like Harry Frankfurt (1969, 1971), have asked us to imagine a science fiction example such that were a subject to show inclination toward a choice contrary to the wishes of a controller, who has the power to control that choice, the controller would intervene to ensure that the subject chooses in accord with the controller's intention. Carl Ginet (1996), as well as others, most notably, Peter van Inwagen (1983), has argued that under certain conditions of causal laws, we are deluded when we think we could have chosen otherwise than we did. But those views are consistent with the minimal claim that we *accept* that we have alternatives, even if we are deceived or deluded. Our acceptance of having alternatives, whether right or wrong, is part and parcel of our own acceptance that our choice is free.

Justification

However, a question remains about whether what we accept is true or false and whether we are justified in accepting that it is true. Thomas Reid (1985) argued that since we inevitably are confronted with situations of choice requiring deliberation, we are equally inevitably confronted with the conviction that we have alternatives. That conviction according to Reid is that we have active power over how we choose between alternative courses of action. Reid concludes that is a conviction of common sense. He compares it to the beliefs that we have in the existence of an external world we distinctly perceive and to the belief that those events that we distinctly remember really did occur. He acknowledges that we are fallible in such beliefs, that we sometimes actually are in error in specific cases, but that is a general feature of belief. The argument that employs the premise—if we can err in a conviction, then we are not justified in that conviction—would lead to total skepticism. We can always err. Infallible belief is a will-o'-the-wisp. It must be acknowledged that not all inevitable beliefs are justified. However, those beliefs that are inevitable in our practical and scientific affairs should be considered justified to accept until evidence shows them to be false. The justification for accepting such beliefs is not that they are proved by argument. They arise in us naturally. The skeptic, Reid (1785) suggested Hume (1739) was among them, who argues against the existence of the external world, for example, and makes war with that conviction in speculation, will find that he believes what the rest of us believe when he leaves his study, as Hume acknowledged. The same can be said of the person who argues against accepting the belief that he is free to choose, for the person is immediately confronted with the choice of whether to continue to spend time arguing against that freedom or turn to other matters. The belief in options inevitably confronts the skeptic of optionality.

Is Reid right in concluding such inevitable beliefs are justified? In my terminology, we can raise the metalevel question—Are we justified in accepting such beliefs? Are the convictions rational? In short, we have arrived at a fundamental question of epistemology. A former colleague of mine, John Pollock, suggested in conversation that if we cannot help believing something, then we are justified in believing it. The argument rests on the assumption that if we cannot help doing something, or believing something, then it follows that we cannot blame a person for doing it as being unjustified. The line is tempting. But the conclusion that we are not wrong or unjustified in doing something does not, unfortunately, entail that we are right or justified. There is a logically open neutral space, concerning peer group disagreement (Lehrer 2011), between not being unjustified and being justified, namely, being neither. The question of justification remains unsettled. If we turn to the metalevel of acceptance and rejection, the open alternative becomes more apparent. We might consider the first-order belief and decide that we have no preference for choosing to accept the belief over rejecting it and do neither. At the level of reflecting on freedom of choice, we are asking a question about power. Do we have the power to choose between options so that whatever we choose, we had the power to choose otherwise? In the modern vernacular, confronted with a choice, I will be convinced that I have leeway, that it is up to me what course of action I choose. Is the conviction justified?

Determinism and Power Preference

The connection between the truth of the claims of the causal order, of determinism in terms of laws of nature, will be discussed in later chapters. I shall there defend the claim that the ultimate explanation for choice is a special form of preference, what I call a *power preference*, and conclude that this claim is logically consistent with the thesis of determinism. An argument for inconsistency combined with determinism is an objection that might defeat an initial justification for the claim of freedom of choice. Is it more reasonable to accept that objection than to accept the belief in freedom? That is an important philosophical question about whether the belief is initially justified. Is the justification defeated by arguments for the truth of determinism and the thesis that this truth is inconsistent with the claim of freedom of choice? But here

I wish to consider whether there is evidence to provide initial justification for accepting the belief that we have the freedom and, as Reid (1895) puts it, the active power to choose between alternatives.

What is the evidence? As Reid puts the matter, the belief arises from our faculties by which we discern truth from error. So either our faculties are fallacious and provide us with no guide to truth, or they provide us with a trustworthy guide to discern truth from error. The pursuit of truth in science or in practical affairs assumes that we have the capacity of our faculties to obtain it. Reid thought of faculties as inborn capacities that we develop with experience. I assume that the shift from the first-order system of belief and desire to the higher-order systems of evaluation is one of our capacities. The implication for reasonableness and evidence of this assumption is profound. Positive evaluation is evidence of truth. Let us return to our example of deliberate choice. I choose between the alternatives of writing or painting this afternoon. I am currently sitting before my computer writing. I stop to consider whether I want to go on or turn to painting. I have to be in the right frame of mind to paint, to allow myself to disappear in the process, applying the medium to express some inchoate feeling or intuition. I look at the last painting on my wall and consider whether I am ready for the process of creating by letting go of the world of words and turn to the world of sense and feeling. To write or paint now: that is the question. However I answer the question, I will have had the other option. Excuse me, I have decided to paint. I will be back.

I have returned to write, but not at the time when I decided to paint, 2:37 p.m. in Tucson. I had the option of writing at that time; I could have continued to write but stopped and deliberated whether to continue or to paint instead. I painted. Figure 1.1 is a black-and-white print of my painting of me contemplating my ultimate freedom in the desert.

The example illustrates the conviction of optionality in choice. It is important to notice the capacity to choose in this way develops with experience. The infant has a capacity, but like the capacity

Figure 1.1 *A View of My Path*, by Keith Lehrer

to walk, it requires a period of experience to develop. Experience teaches me how to engage freedom of choice responding to options. That freedom involves the consideration of alternatives, or, if it occurs without reflection, at least a background conviction of alternatives. Moreover, experience teaches us to modify how we choose. We learn to reflect on past choices ill made, and we learn from the reflection on our mistakes to change how we choose. We think, "That choice was awful. I should have chosen otherwise!" It is not only deliberation about future choices that carries with it the conviction of genuine options. Reflection on my past contains the conviction that I could have chosen differently.

Moreover, in addition to the evidence of conviction, there is further evidence of experience of variation in the choice of options. I am often convinced by experience that in the relevantly similar circumstances I sometimes choose one way and sometimes another. That evidence, which is too robust to insist upon here as I did previously (Lehrer 1966a), further supports the conviction of an ability to choose in different ways between the same options. It is an exercise of a power of preference. The conviction of active power to choose between alternatives in the light of reason and experience reveals our reflective freedom of choice.

Evidence

Let me put the point more precisely in terms of evidence. I have argued for the inevitability of our conviction of the freedom of choice. I am proposing with Reid that although argument can create the weight of evidence, there is more to evidence than argument supplies. Acceptance of something, as we exercise of our intellectual capacities of evaluating first-order responses in the light of reason and experience, gives some weight of evidence to what we accept. Reid argued that the convictions of common sense that arise in this manner are original results of our faculties and have the highest degree of evidence as they arise. For him, their justification is their birthright. I prefer a more modest conclusion about such inevitable beliefs and evidence. I argued (2011) that the conviction of our freedom of choice arising from the exercise of our capacities to evaluate the truth of it offers some evidence in favor of it. Our accepting it on the basis of our higher-order evaluation based on experience is in itself evidence. My conclusion is this: it is more reasonable on the basis of the evidence of experience to accept that we have freedom of choice than to accept the denial of this.

I note further, what I have argued earlier, and will later develop, that this implies that the claim of freedom of choice is more probable than its denial on the basis of our evidence. If you agree that the evidence described makes it more probable that we have freedom of choice but are inclined to argue that such evidence does not refute the claim that human choice is determined by the laws of nature, I agree with you. Your conclusion should be that the evidence of freedom makes freedom of choice probable but fails to refute determinism. Then you should take the next logical step and follow me (Lehrer 1966a) in concluding that freedom of choice is logically consistent with determinism. For if freedom of choice entails the falsity of determinism, then evidence that makes freedom probable must, by the logic of probability, make the falsity of determinism probable. I leave you to draw the conclusion. Freedom and determinism are logically consistent. I will elaborate the argument in later chapters.

Reason and Power Preference

However, the promise of this opening chapter is an account of the connection between preferences among options leading to freedom of choice and the role of reason in the formation of preferences. My fundamental claim is this: the choice of how we reason about alternatives to form preferences is itself an expression of a preference. This may seem odd because you may be inclined to think in linear fashion about a person reasoning about the merit of alternatives and forming a preference about what to choose as a result. I concede this is a natural way to think about reason and choice, but it ignores the question of how we choose to reason in one way rather than another. How are we to explain the weight that we give to one line of reasoning over another in forming preference? The question arises—What is the relation between the preference for a choice of action and the preference for a line of reasoning concerning the choice? Sometimes the preference for a line of reasoning relevant to a preference for a choice of action precedes it, which one might naturally assume as routine rational choice. Sometimes, however, preference for a line of reasoning arises at the same time as the preference for the choice of action, which may arise in a novel or problematic choice. For example, Greta is trying to evoke higher-order consideration of her scientific reasoning in her audience of leaders. Suppose that a member of the audience who is open to change of preference, call him C, is appreciative of Greta's speech. She succeeds in convincing C to change his preference. C's preference for the line of reasoning Greta affirms as well as his preference for choosing G, a policy of the Greens, may occur at the same time as positive evaluation of the reasoning in her speech. Moreover, sometimes the preference for a line of reasoning may arise subsequent to the choice as a defense of the preference concerning the choice of action. If C is provoked by Greta's speech to suddenly prefer to choose G, he may afterward prefer her line of reasoning in defense of his preference for G.

All of these connections between preferences over choices and preferences over lines of reasoning are explained in terms of higher-order consideration of preferences, evaluations, and the formation of a power preference. Higher-order consideration reveals a higher order of preference in agency and the expression of our active power. There will be conflict among desires concerning our choice of actions, re-expressed at a higher level as conflict among preferences representing higher-order evaluation of those desires. Similarly, there will be conflict among desires to follow one line of reasoning represented at a higher level as well as conflict between preferences for choosing one line of reasoning or another. As we move to a higher level, the first-order desires for action and lines of reasoning will be re-represented in a higher-level system to form a preference and a power preference. I shall turn to an examination of this connection between preferring a line of reasoning and preferring a choice of action in a later chapter.

Conflict among Preferences

Now a natural question arises of how conflict among preferences can be resolved at the higher level. One answer is that a higher-order preference should resolve the conflict by aligning desires in favor of the same course of action, as Frankfurt (1971) has proposed. However, preferences of various levels that are in conflict may be retained, contrary to Frankfurt, while a higher-order preference for the entire structure of preferences including a first-order preference for an action governs choice for the action. Returning to the example of Greta and the government representatives at the climate summit, we can imagine a conflict among preferences on the part of an anonymous delegate, D. A policy is proposed by a consortium of delegates on behalf of a modest policy M to reduce CO_2 emissions. D initially prefers to vote for that policy. However, hearing Greta, reminding him in a vivid way of what he knows about climate change and his responsibility for future effects, he would prefer at a second level to prefer a stronger green policy SG. SG is the policy Greta advocates to radically reduce CO_2. But, in fact, his first-order preference for the modest policy M remains. Perhaps that is because, as he reflects about his second-level preference for having a preference for SG rather than M, he has a third-order-level preference for conforming his preference structure to the directions of his government, and, therefore, a preference not to have the preference for SG. I consider it a mistake to suppose that D simply lines up all his preferences consistently in line with choosing M. The first-order preference for M is admittedly revealed in his choice that leads Greta to her "How dare you!" rhetoric. That remark is intended to provoke the listeners to change their first-order preferences or, at least, to acknowledge to themselves their responsibility for not having a first-order preference for SG.

The force of D retaining the second-order preference for SG is that D has the power to alter his first-order preference M and make the second-order preference dominate the first-order preference, becoming the first-order preference. The second-order preference might dominate the first-order preference were it not for the third-order preference against the second-order preference expressing commitment to the wishes of his government for M. I suppose D is a man of conscience who recognizes the conflict among his preferences, knows that M is ineffective in dealing with climate change, even though he votes for M. It is up to him what preference structure he maintains. His preference structure, I suppose, represents both his conflict of preference and his freedom of choice, as Greta's rhetoric implies. She implies that he has the power to prefer and choose whether to vote for policy M or policy SG, and her remark implies that it is within his power whether he aligns his preference against his government's directions or not. He is the agent of his preferences, and, as I would add, of the structure and ordering of his preferences.

What ensures that the preference structure is in his power and that he is the agent of it? The answer I have defended elsewhere and will now elaborate completes the account of ultimate preference and ultimate freedom as a result. The person has a special preference for the preferences in his preference structure and for his preference of choosing M among conflicting preferences. I have called that a *power preference*. It is a preference for the full structure of preferences at various levels concerning choosing M. Here are the preferences in the preference structure PSM that D has concerning choosing M:

1. D has a first-order preference for choosing M.
2. D has a second-level preference, 2, for not having preference 1 but for choosing SG instead based on concern for climate change.
3. D has a third-order preference, 3, for not having the second-order preference 2, against having the first-order preference 1 because of a preference for M based on his loyalty to his government's directions.
4. D has power preference for preferring the preference structure PSM including all the preferences concerning choosing M, including 1–3 and 4 itself.

The power preference, 4, has the feature that, since it is itself a preference concerning choosing M, it is a preference in the preference structure as well. The power preference, therefore, loops back onto itself. It is a preference for itself as well as for the other preferences in the preference structure concerning M. The power preference ends a potential regress of higher-order preferences and, at the same time, acknowledges the conflict between preferences.

Moreover, if Greta and we are justified in thinking that it is up to D how he chooses, then he must have the preference structure including the power preference because he prefers to have it. If he is a puppet of another, the response of D to Greta would be, he had no choice. If it is up to him how he chooses, as we and she think, then he must have the power preference for his preference structure leading to choosing M *because* he prefers to have it. That is why he has ultimate freedom of choice.

Power Preference and Explanation

I shall examine the details of this role of a power preference to empower the agent in a later chapter. I note here, however, that to say a person has a preference because he prefers to have it is a claim about the primary explanation of the choice. He chooses because of a preference to so choose, and that preference is explained by a power preference for all his preferences concerning the choice. The power preference must be the primary explanation, one that would suffice to explain the choice without appeal to earlier history. He chooses as he does because of what he prefers now, and he prefers what he does now because of his power preference for his preferences now. The power preference is a preference for itself and is both self-referential and self-explanatory. It is, of course, necessary to add that if the person has genuine freedom of choice, then he could have chosen otherwise. I shall clarify this later but note that just as it is sufficient for his choosing that his choice is explained by a power preference for that choice, so it would be sufficient for his choosing otherwise than choosing that way. Choosing otherwise would be explained by a power preference for his choosing otherwise. Whatever he chooses, whether for the action or against it, the primary explanation would be a power preference for the choice. We shall discover that as this suffices for ultimate freedom of choice, it resolves a traditional problem about the connection between freedom of choice and a scientific account of human choice. We leave the details for later.

We are closing in on a sufficient condition for ultimate freedom. However, before ending this chapter, we must return to the relationship between reason and choice. Just as D chooses from his preferences, so his preferences will result from reasoning, for example, about the climate as well as about the directions he has received, and perhaps, the financial costs of the stronger choice, SG. If the choice is explained by the power preference, what about the role of reasoning for those preferences? The answer I shall defend is that the choice of reasons, what counts as a reason for him to form a preference, is itself the result of preference and a power preference explaining why he accepts the reasoning as he does. Sometimes the choice of a line of reasoning concerning an action may precede the action, but sometimes it may occur at the same time. Preference for a line of reasoning concerning an action may itself contain conflict. A power preference for the preference structure concerning the line of reasoning may explain why the line of reasoning is chosen.

Reason and Choice

This leaves us with a question about the relation between the power preference for the choice of action and the power preference for the line of reasoning. They might be the same. The choice of a line of reasoning concerning a choice may settle the choice. In that case, the power preference for the choice of a line of reasoning concerning an action and the power preference for the choice of action may be one and the same. If that seems odd, consider an important choice. There is a fabricated story, or maybe a joke, about the great decision theorist Professor Luce as he was writing his famous work on decision theory with Raiffa (Luce and Raiffa 1957), according to which rational choice was made in terms of filling in utilities and preference in a matrix and applying expected utility theory to determine the rational choice. As the story goes, Luce was working with Raiffa at Harvard when he received an offer from the new campus at Irvine at the University of California. The choice was difficult. Irvine was offering the opportunity for him to run his own unit, a free hand, rather than fitting into the traditional Harvard structure. There were personal matters involved. There was the great status of Harvard. There was the beautiful beach community near Irvine and wonderful weather to consider as he sat in the gloom of a Cambridge winter. Luce was finding it very difficult to decide. A graduate student, also a confidant, got weary of the indecision and remarked, "You know how to decide. You fill in the matrix of utilities and calculate." Luce is reported to have replied, "This is serious, you know." Only a good story perhaps. But it may illustrate that the preference over a choice and over how to reason about a choice may be inseparable. My conclusion is that forming a power preference about a choice and about a line of reasoning about the choice may be inseparable. So, the power preference may explain at the same time the preference concerning a line of reasoning about choice and the preference about the choice itself. It may tie both in an explanatory loop of a power preference that places both within the power of the agent. The explanatory power of a power preference may explain agency about reason and preference.

Some philosophers, notably recently Nomy Arpaly and Timothy Schroeder (2015) and somewhat earlier Kadri Vihvelin (2000), sometimes called *agent causation theorists*, have argued that freedom of choice requires that the agent be the cause of choice.

What more could be required to make an agent the cause of his choice than that his power preferences over preferences and reasoning are ones he has *because* he prefers to have them?

I hope that the foregoing discourse will provoke questions answered in the chapters to come.

2
Freedom of Choice
Source and Leeway

In this chapter my aim is to further elaborate a conception of freedom of choice resulting from higher-level preference, most notably a power preference over a structure of preference. Here is the account of ultimate freedom of choice I seek to defend:

> A person S who chooses A has ultimate freedom of choice if (i) she prefers to choose A and, whatever higher-order preferences the person has concerning preferences pertaining to choosing A, she prefers to have those preferences in a power preference, (ii) she prefers, as a power preference pertaining to A, to have her preference structure pertaining to A, and (iii) the primary explanation for her choosing A is her power preference expressing her active power of preference.

I shall argue that this ultimate freedom of choice is at the same time both (i) what is known as a *source* theory of freedom (Frankfurt 1971), initially controverted by Marjory Naylor (1984) and developed by Carolina Sartorio (2016), affirming that the choice is an expression of freedom when it expresses an ultimate preference and (ii) a traditional leeway theory of freedom, when ultimate freedom entails that the person has alternative possibilities of choice and preference. Ultimate freedom combines a source theory with a leeway theory of freedom in accord with Kevin Timpe (2012). Before turning to an elaboration of freedom of choice, it is important to distinguish choice from other forms of response. There are many actions that are not choices exercising freedom of choice over options because attention to options is not available. Indeed, many of our actions are going to be immediate fast responses, first-order responses, what Kahneman calls system 1 responses, that lack attention to alternative courses of action that could lead to reflective consideration of them and deliberation. They are spontaneous responses that are activated below the level of attention to alternatives. Some are even below the level of consciousness of what we are doing or why we are doing it. We often act too quickly to ponder why we acted that way, or to consider other ways of acting.

Anna Rothschild of *Nova* with F. Jabr (Robinson 2020) presented a fascinating program about mold slimes, single-cell organisms, that respond in ways considered intelligent, finding their way through mazes, seeming to remember dead ends, and even transferring the information to other slime molds. There is a lot of intelligent behavior of our own that resembles how the slime mold moves. We respond unreflectively to external and internal impulses in ways that are intelligent and, as Kahneman notes, played a role in our survival as a species. I recall, as an illustration, a program in which Carl Sagan claimed that a part of our brain is a residue of the reptilian brain that controls our responses. I was disposed to doubt his conclusion that a reptilian part of my brain controlled my responses. Then I went hiking in the desert. A noise startled me and, unthinking, I ran a few steps, turned around, and looked. It was the rattle of a rattlesnake, though I had not consciously identified it as such. Indeed, I do not think I had ever heard the rattle of a rattlesnake before. And then I thought of how lizards respond when startled. My response felt reflexive, perhaps reptilian, like that of a lizard.

Some of our fast responses are not reflexes, though they may be rapid first-level reactions. I think that many of our responses are these first-level fast reactions. We may not think of them as things we do of our free will. An act of will, assuming that implies attentive choice to options, is actually lacking. The spontaneity of such responses, when not reflexive, may give us a feeling of freedom, of free will. They may be ingrained habits or forms of association. We often describe spontaneous behavior as fully in accord with desire, as things we do of our own free will. We may judge the behavior of others performed in such a spontaneous manner as things they have done of their own free will. This is probably the result of what Peter Strawson (1962) and Michael McKenna (2012) as well as Gary Watson (1987) modifying Strawson, described as our reactive attitudes to such behavior based on morals. There is often controversy in such attributions. See, for example, Joseph Keim Campbell (2017). My goal here is to identify the notion of freedom of choice, which is the focus of this work. The point I am making here is that spontaneous fast response, whether reflex, conditioned response, habit, or just first-level or system 1 reaction, is not choice under informed optionality. Put another way, these fast responses are ones that block or simply fail to engage the influence of appropriate reasoning based on background information. Higher-level preference based on accepted reasoning about options is blocked as a result of fast response, or if there is any awareness of reasoning, it is bracketed off in the manner of Husserl (1989) to provide phenomenological clarity. Desire drives one to respond without the higher-order evaluation of the desire or related beliefs based on reasoning about the consequences of a fast response.

Preferences over Preferences and Power Preferences

Choice, as I have indicated, is a choice among options of which one is aware, so that we may say the person intentionally chose her action as an option knowing what she was doing or not doing. As indicated in the last chapter, such choice reveals a higher-order preference structure including a power preference for the preference structure over a choice of an action A with a first-level preference for A rather than an option to prefer some alternative. I note here that many preferences over preferences are preferences at higher levels that may be indexed semantically or conceptually for a specific level. Assume an initial first-level preference for a choice of action A, indexed level 1. A preference concerning that preference, whether supporting or conflicting, would be a level 2 preference. A preference concerning that preference would be a level 3 preference, and so forth to higher levels of preference. However, a power preference over all levels of preference in the preference structure of levels of preference is level ambiguous, even if preferences are limited to level 1 and a power preference over it. The power preference cannot be indexed to a level, for two reasons. The obvious reason is that there is no fixed number of levels in all preference structures. That ambiguity could be in principle dealt with by assigning power preferences a variety of level indices depending on the other levels of preference if the preferences have a finite number of levels.

But that leaves two problems. One is that the levels of preference might be unlimited, infinite. Note that preference is a higher-order functional state that may be computationally specified for the agent to answer the question of whether he prefers a preference at a given level within an infinity of levels. (This infinity of levels could be one in which there is a finite pattern, even with conflicts, that could be computationally repeated.) However, the more critical problem to assigning a level to a power preference for preferences in a preference structure over a choice of a specific action A is that it is itself a preference in the preference structure over A, and therefore a preference for itself. It is a self-referential and, I shall argue, a self-explanatory preference. We could assign a variety of level numbers to power preferences depending on the number of other levels of preferences in the preference structure, perhaps even infinity for some. But that would conceal, rather than clarify, the role of a power preference, which has a self-referential and self-explanatory role over the variety of choices and preference structures. It would formally conceal the point that power preferences express and explain what Thomas Reid (1985) called the *active power* of the agent over choices and the freedom thereof.

To return to my example in the previous chapter, my choice to write may be the preference over other options like painting, my hobby. However, I might have a second-level preference not to have the first-level preference, perhaps motivated by a desire not to be so obsessive about writing about the philosophy of freedom and to enjoy the pleasure of expressing myself in painting. I might even have a third-level preference not to have that second-level preference, perhaps motivated by reflection on the long-range satisfactions of completing my writing projects in philosophy. Of course, my first-level preference is to write my philosophy, and my power preference for the structure of preferences including that first-level preference is sufficient to resolve conflict in favor of choosing to write this chapter. The effect of the other conflicting higher-level preference to paint for pleasure may be that it will become effective another time that would afford me the choice of painting. We do not have to align all our preferences in favor of a first-level preference to choose that preference or to be free in that choice. Moreover, the power preference over the first-level preference for freedom of choice of action from a profile may suffice without other higher-level preferences.

Power Preference in Freedom of Choice

It is essential to immediately clarify the role of the power preference in freedom of choice. The explanatory role is essential for the sufficiency of the power preference in freedom of choice. The power preference is self-referential and self-explanatory because it provides an explanation of why the person has the preferences in the preference structure, including the decisive first-order preference. The answer to the question why the person has the preferences in the preference structure is that she prefers to have them. Moreover, the same answer is available concerning why the person has the power preference itself, namely, that she prefers to have it. That is important for the sufficiency of a power preference to supply freedom of choice, but it is not adequate for that freedom. The reason is that a self-explanatory account of the preference does not ensure that it is the primary explanation for the choice even in terms of the present conditions of choice. For those conditions may include concealed manipulation of the preference structure, including the power preference. If someone listening to Greta Thunberg, mentioned in the earlier chapter arguing for concern about climate change, is controlled or manipulated by an opponent of such concern, it is the control of choice by the other that may be the primary explanation of choice. Contrary to the existential take of Jean-Paul Sartre (1956), our consciousness of our choice can be controlled by another, even another acting concealed from our experience, deceiving us into thinking our choice is free. The control of the other may extend to control over our power preferences and abrogate the role of the power preference as the primary explanation of choice.

What is required for the power preference to be the primary explanation? To answer the question, one must first note that explanations may extend into the past. I acknowledge the scientific importance of such extension of explanations. However, and here I am perhaps influenced by the existential point of view, I think the essence of explanation of how a person chooses now is contained in the present, perhaps the specious present. We love narratives, and the narratives of explanation may explain the power preference. But the power preference may be the primary explanation of the choice, nonetheless. That will result when the power preference is adequate to explain the choice without appeal to further explanations, even explanations of how the power preference itself arose. In short, sometimes the power preference will be adequate to explain why the person chooses as she does at the present moment without appeal to other conditions from the past. Freedom here and now depends on active power exerted here and now. The active power of agency is expressed by the standalone adequacy of the power preference to explain the choice.

Ultimate Explanation of Preference

What is required for this standalone explanatory adequacy of the power preference? The power preference must dominate explanation in the conditions and powers of the agent at the moment of choice. Explanations proliferate temporally and spatially, with scientific benefit. But when the role of the power preference in explanation of choice here and now is adequate and dominant without appeal to other explanations, I shall say that explanation is *ultimate*. When I say it is ultimate, I mean that the exercise of the power of preference here and now is essential as well as adequate without appeal to other explanatory factors past or present. When the power preference is an ultimate explanation, that means the power preference is essential to explanation of freedom of choice, and other explanations are inadequate to explain the choice. This is the account that is needed to ensure that manipulation, coercion, or other factors do not explain the choice. I express this by saying that the power preference is the *ultimate* explanation, ending levels of preference and tying them together in an explanatory loop. That is an *ultimate preference*. When the power preference for choice is the ultimate explanation for what is chosen and, therefore, an ultimate preference, it is sufficient for freedom of choice.

The conception of a power preference as ultimate requires meeting a basic objection that has been central to the discussion of compatibilism, namely, that no preference is ultimate in the sense suggested. The premise behind the objection is that determinism implies that all choice is explained by the past given the laws of nature. Though I wish to delay my discussion and defense of compatibilism described as the consistency thesis to a later chapter, it is essential here to clarify the notion of ultimate preference. I have noted that the power preference is ultimate in the sense that it is a preference that ends a regress of higher-order preferences concerning a choice about an action A and other options that exclude A. In addition, if the power preference is an ultimate preference, an ultimate explanation of the choice, then it must be essential and dominate other explanations. Dominating and being essential entails that other explanations are inadequate to explain the choice.

Explanation and Nomological Connection

Now, this might sound like embracing a libertarian view denying nomological determinism entailing a deductive chain from past events and nomological connection of scientific laws entailing the choice from the past. However, that is not a consequence of affirming the ultimate explanation of choice by a power preference in freedom of choice. The reason is twofold. First, nomological deduction does not entail explanation. Second, explanation is not transitive. Consequently, it is consistent to maintain at the same time that everything has an explanation, including the power preference that explains the choice, even though the power preference is an ultimate explanation of the choice. It is consistent to affirm that a power preference has an explanation in terms of the past and scientific laws but, at the same time, to deny that what explains the power preference, therefore, explains the choice. The consistency is a logical consequence of the failure of general transitivity of explanation. Transitivity is not a universal or logical feature of explanation.

Here are the arguments for my claims that nomological deduction is insufficient for explanation and that general transitivity of explanation fails. Concerning the insufficiency of explanation, Sylvain Bromberger (1965) proved many years ago that nomological deduction is not sufficient for explanation. In reply to Carl Hempel (1962), Bromberger showed that nomological deduction of an event from laws and conditions does not entail explanation. Bromberger (1965, 1993) argued convincingly, and I follow him, that an explanation is an answer to a *why-question*. Nomological deduction may fail to answer a *why-question*. An explanation of a person's choice to do A must answer the question, Why did the person choose to do A? There may be many conditions (some remote, like having been born, and some present, like a supply of oxygen) that are necessary for the person's choosing as she does, or even sufficient, but that does not answer the question of *why* she chose as she did. It is something about our active power, something about our power preferences, that I propose as an ultimate explanation of free choice.

Examples are important, and here is one adopted from Bromberger. His example was the application of the Pythagorean theorem construed as an empirical hypothesis about spatial relations. If you deduce the length of a distance between two objects triangulating a right triangle from some arbitrary object with a known distance from each of the two objects using the Pythagorean theorem, you will not, in spite of nomological deduction, have explained why the two objects are the calculated distance from each other. An example modified to the issue of choice may make this clear. Suppose a woman is standing in front of a man threatening her with gun. I may want you to explain why she chooses to stand at that distance from the man. Suppose you respond that it easy to explain this, marking a spot on the ground that forms a right triangle from the woman and the man with known distances from the spot to the man, m, and to the woman, w. You then compute the distance, d, of the woman from the man, by the Pythagorean theorem, $d^2 = w^2 + m^2$. But that does not explain why the woman is standing that distance from the man threatening her with a gun even though the distance is deduced from an empirical principle concerning spatial relations on earth. Deduction of a conclusion from an empirical law does entail an explanation of why the conclusion is true.

Now let us consider why the general assumption of transitivity of explanation is fallacious. Here is my example. If explanation were transitive, then ipso facto anything that explained my power preference over a choice would explain the choice. The examples of intransitivity are robust. Here is one. I am driving to keep an appointment with you at 7:00 p.m. at my favorite restaurant, Le Crocodile in Vancouver. On the way, I run over a nail and get a flat in the front left tire. I then change the tire and arrive on time at Le Crocodile. My running over a nail and getting a flat tire explains why I change the front left tire. My changing the front left tire explains why I arrive at Le Crocodile on time. But running over a nail and getting a flat left tire do not explain why I arrive at Le Crocodile on time. The general inference from the statement "A explains B" and "B explains C" to "A explains C" I call the *transitivity fallacy*.

Ultimate Preference and Freedom of Choice

Once we note that it is a fallacy, we can understand why conditions that manipulate my preferences to explain why I choose A preclude the preferences from being the ultimate explanation of the choice. If manipulation explains my choice, then my preference is not an ultimate explanation. When the power preference explains my choice without being the result of manipulation, coercion, or obsession, to mention only a few conditions that might interfere with freedom of choice, the power preference is adequate, by itself, to explain my choice. Other explanations are inessential and fail to answer the question of why I chose what I did when my choice was free. I exercised freedom of choice because my power preference was the ultimate explanation of the choice. Again, note that my power preference may have an explanation, even when I exercise freedom of choice, but the explanation for the power preference will not be what explains the choice. The power preference, as an ultimate preference, stands alone as an adequate explanation of the choice.

I am here advancing the view that freedom of choice depends on what explains it. Once we take explanation as central to understanding of freedom of choice, we obtain an understanding of the special role of preference, of a power preference, in explaining freedom. The power preference is an ultimate preference that stands alone without appeal to other conditions in the explanation of the choice. That makes the choice one of the active power of the agent expressed in the power preference. We can also understand why the counterexamples to freedom of choice work, and, at the same time, why nomological deduction of choice does not destroy freedom. The explanation of choice by preference must be ultimate to entail that the choice was free. Counterexamples to accounts of freedom of choice explain the choice in terms of some factor other than preference of the agent. Examples are manipulation, obsession, and so forth. An ultimate explanation of choice from a power preference blocks the counterexamples. Moreover, nomological deduction, useful for scientific inference, does not entail explanation of the choice and leaves open the power preference as the ultimate explanation of the choice. That makes the power preference an ultimate preference.

Desire and Preference: Frankfurt's Example

It may be useful to contrast the present view of a power preference as ultimate explanation with the work of Frankfurt (1971). His important work about free will focused on an argument to the effect that an agent may act of his or her own free will though he could not have chosen otherwise. Frankfurt's reason was that the will of the agent, Joe, may be fully aligned with Joe's first-order desire for action A he acts on, even though, unknown to Joe, there is an external agent, Black, with the power to intervene and produce the desire to do A in Joe if there was any sign of Joe's having a desire not to do A. In this situation Black, who can read the signs of what Joe desires, does not intervene in any way because Joe desires to do A of his own accord. However, the powers of Black, though not exercised, entail that Joe could not have desired not to do A nor to act on such a desire. Frankfurt (1988) argues Joe, doing A, acted of his own free will when his desire is wholehearted and aligns with his higher-order desires, even though Joe lacked the alternative not to do A.

To contrast Frankfurt's notion of free will with my account of freedom of choice, note that Joe would be deceived if he thought he had freedom of choice. If Joe thinks he has freedom of choice, then he thinks that his preference to do A is a preference over a profile of alternatives that includes not doing A. Moreover, and this is the crucial point, he thinks that whatever his determining preference, whether for doing A or not, that preference would be explained by an expression of his active power of preference, that is, by his power preference for his choice.

Frankfurt rests the case for freedom of will on desire and higher-order desire. I argue by contrast that freedom of choice transcends a first-order response based on desire and depends on a higher-order power preference. Frankfurt's account involves higher-level desires aligned with the first-order desires to support his argument concerning acts of free will without being able to do otherwise. I oppose my account of freedom of choice based on higher-order preference to his account of free will based on higher-order desire. I acknowledge, however, that my account of higher-order preference is indebted to Frankfurt's brilliant account of higher-order desire, though it differs from it in a crucial way. Imagine, in line with my account so far, that a power preference is a preference over preferences containing both the chosen action A and the alternative of not doing A. The power preference would cover what an agent thinks of as alternatives to A, *including not doing A*. If the agent conceives of himself as having freedom of choice, then he thinks that whatever he chooses, whether A or not A, will be explained by his preference for that choice. In examples where some external agent like Black is empowered to intervene and manipulate the preferences of the agent, Joe for example, the agent is deceived about his or her freedom of choice. The agent *thinks* that however he chooses, or would choose, his choice is adequately explained by his preference. In my terms, he thinks the power preference will be the ultimate preference of his choice. To do justice to Frankfurt, we may acknowledge that the agent will correctly think he does what he wills, which Frankfurt describes as acting of his own free will, but he will be deceived if he thinks that he has freedom of choice. His preference will not be an ultimate preference yielding ultimate freedom.

In classical examples of manipulation, the agent will be wrong about his freedom because his choice will be explained by the direct exercise of manipulation. In Frankfurt-style examples the agent will be deceived as well, however. The counterfactual intervener, Black, though he does not intervene, would intervene if he knew the agent, Joe, were to prefer not to choose A and would manipulate Joe's preferences so Joe chooses A. Joe would be mistaken in such examples in thinking that his preference would be the primary explanation, the ultimate explanation of his choice, no matter what he chooses. If he were to choose other than A, the counterfactual intervener, Black, would have to change his plan to allow Joe to choose other than A because Black's original plan is to insure Joe will choose A. Therefore, Black's *change of plan* must be included to explain Joe's choosing other than A if he were to do that instead of choosing A. Black's change of plan would be essential to any adequate explanation of Joe being allowed by Black to choose to do otherwise. This observation is intended, not as refutation of Frankfurt, but rather to reveal a subtle difference between an account of free will based on desire, Frankfurt's, and the present account of freedom of choice based on preference and a power preference.

Thus, if the power preference is the ultimate preference for what the agent chooses, then the agent has freedom to choose another option. That freedom entails that whatever the agent chooses, he or she could have chosen otherwise. That is the power of the ultimate preference over a profile of preference options. The profile includes the alternative of choosing other than what he actually chooses. The power preference as an ultimate preference of choice explains why the choice is a free choice, up to the agent as he or she conceives of the choice. Explanation of choice reveals whether the choice is free. An ultimate power preference is intended to ensure freedom of choice that rules out explanation of choice leading to action from manipulation, coercion or even irresistible first-order impulses and desires. When such impulses and desires block the active power of the agent, then preference, including power preference, is not the ultimate explanation of the choice. When the power preference is the ultimate explanation of choice, then the influence of the higher level is unblocked and dominates lower-level response.

Could Have Done Otherwise: Accessible Possible Worlds

To complete this account of freedom of choice, the role of higher-order states of reasoning in preference is required. The role of such reasoning will be the subject of the next chapters. However, the claim that the ultimate preference of an agent for choosing A entails the modal claim that agent *could* have chosen otherwise requires further defense. I have claimed that when a power preference is the ultimate explanation for a choice of A, the first-order preference is a preference over a profile of alternatives. As the ultimate explanation for the choice of A, the power preference is a preference for A over the alternatives. But we must account for the counterfactual claim that the agent could have chosen the other alternatives. I have said that if the ultimate explanation for choosing A is the power preference for choosing A, then if the agent had chosen otherwise, the power preference would be the ultimate explanation for that choice instead. So, if preference is the ultimate explanation for choice, then nothing makes the person choose in that way. If any factor other than the power preference were to make her choose as she does, that factor would be the explanation for the choice. If nothing else makes her choose as she does, then she could have chosen otherwise. The ultimate explanation of power preference ensures it was up to her how she chose. She could have chosen otherwise.

Since the notion of what a person could have done is a modal notion, it might be illuminating to think about what a person could have chosen, though she did not in the actual world, as being equivalent to what she chooses to do in another possible world. I have earlier explored a possible worlds analysis of saying that a person could have chosen otherwise in the actual world as equivalent to saying that there is some possible world accessible to her from the actual world in which she chooses otherwise than she did in the actual world. What makes the possible world *accessible* in which she chooses some alternative B other than A, her choice in the actual world? We must rule out, I argued, worlds in which she has some advantage for choosing B that she lacks in the actual world. So, the natural proposal is that there is some possible world in which she had no advantages for choosing B instead of A in the accessible possible world, W_{AP}, she lacks in the actual world W_a. To ensure that W_{AP} is as much like the actual world, W_a, given that the agent chooses B instead of A in the possible world, I required that W_{AP} is a world minimally different from the actual world in which the person chooses B instead of A. That is how Pollock (1976) treats subjunctive conditionals. For the present purposes, I shall use Stalnaker's (1968) account of counterfactuals, explicitly formulated as the most similar possible world to the actual world in which the person chooses B instead of A. For details of this account, and to avoid repetition here, I refer you to my earlier work (Lehrer 1976) on "can" and possible worlds.

Possible Worlds and Ultimate Preference

I claimed in the earlier work that the person could have done B instead of A, when, in the actual world, she chose A, is equivalent to the claim that there is a possible world W_{AP} in which the person chooses B instead of A that is the most similar possible world in which she chooses B instead of A with no advantages for choosing B instead of A that she lacked in the actual world. Intuitively, we judge the person could have chosen otherwise if we can imagine her choosing otherwise in a world as similar to ours as we can imagine with no advantages for so choosing that she lacks in the actual world.

This possible world account of what a person could have chosen might seem very different from the ultimate preference account of what a person could have chosen. How does the power preference serving as the ultimate explanation for the preference and choice to do otherwise connect with the idea that a most similar possible world in which the person chooses otherwise must be a world in which the person does not have any advantage for the choice to do otherwise that he lacks in the actual world? The answer is that advantages are connected with explanation. Suppose there is no condition CA that is an advantage needed for a person choosing to do otherwise in the most similar possible world. In that case the lack of CA does not matter for explaining the person's choosing otherwise in the possible world, or the lack of CA does matter for explanation in that world. To say it matters is equivalent to saying that presence of the advantage in the most similar possible world in which the person chooses otherwise is essential to an adequate explanation of the choice. In that case, the power preference fails as an ultimate explanation. Thus, the addition of the ultimate preference theory of freedom of choice adds an account of how the agent must have all the advantages she needs to do B instead of A. If she needs any other advantage to choose B instead of A, then no preference the person has will be an ultimate preference explaining the choice of B instead of A.

In both the earlier paper (Lehrer 1976) and in the present chapter, it is features of the present state of the subject, her power preference, that explain what the person does when she could have done otherwise. Past conditions are not the ultimate explanation of free choices when a person could have preferred and chosen otherwise. It is the present power preference that explains what the person chooses and does so without any need to appeal to the past. If the person had some advantage in the most similar possible world where she does otherwise that she lacked in the actual world, then the presence of the advantage would be a necessary part of the explanation for her choice to do otherwise.

Conclusion: Active Power and Power Preference

In conclusion, then, I note here a clarification of the notion of a *power preference*. I think of a power preference as an expression of an active power to form preferences. I shall in later chapters provide an account of the higher-order reasoning in the formation of preferences and power preferences. Here I note a power preference over a preference to choose A includes, minimally, preference over some alternative to A, call it B, that logically excludes A and may consist simply of refraining from doing A. So, the power preference is not just a preference for choosing to do A, if that is preferred by the agent, but also for, contrary to fact, a preference for a preference for choosing to do B excluding A, if that were preferred instead. In short, the power preference is a preference for whatever the agent prefers to choose in a profile of alternatives targeting A. This is implied by Greta Thunberg in her challenge, "How dare you?" When we exercise freedom of choice, it up to us what we prefer to choose. It is, therefore, in our power, our active power, to choose otherwise. That is the reward and burden of freedom of choice.

3
Reason, Preference, and Freedom

Freedom of choice can be dominated by reason and the action of others. My purpose in this chapter is to set freedom of choice itself free from the bondage of reason and the demands of others. Here is the problem: some philosophers, Kant (1959) most notably, and Fischer (1994) most recently, have said that governing your life by reason or by being responsive to reason is the source of freedom of choice. But there is a paradox concealed in these plausible claims. On the one hand, a person can be enslaved to reason and lack freedom of choice because of this kind of bondage. On the other hand, if reason has no influence on us, and we are not even capable of being governed by reason in what we choose, then it appears that one would be the slave of one's passions or other random influences. Hume (1739) might have written positively about reason being the servant of the passions. There is something odd, however, about the idea that a person who is enslaved by his passions has freedom of choice. The paradox, which I shall call *the paradox of reason*, is that if we are governed by reason in what we choose, then we are in bondage to reason in what we choose, and we lack freedom of choice. Yet, if we are not governed by reason, then we do not govern ourselves in what we choose, and again we lack freedom of choice.

The difficulty for freedom finds a parallel problem in the connection of freedom of choice from the preferences of others. If we are enslaved to satisfy the preferences of others, to conform our preferences to their preferences, we are bound by the preferences of others and lack freedom of choice. On the other hand, if the preferences of others can have no influence on us, if we are not capable of responding to the preferences of others sympathetically, then we are egocentric, blocking the natural response of empathy for others. We might retain egoistic freedom of choice but lack the freedom of humane choice concerning the preferences of others. This problem is closely connected with the paradox of reason. The preferences of others are often reasons for our own preferences. When we are governed by reason, including reasons concerning the preferences of others, the paradox of reason arises again.

The paradox is not a mere sophism of philosophy. At the level of phenomenology, we might feel that if we are governed by reason, then we are constrained by it, and if we are not governed by reason, then we are not in control. Suppose that to be governed by reason is to be moved by rational considerations in how we choose. If being moved by rational considerations is a form of causation, that appears to dominate freedom of choice. Freedom appears bound to reason. Once the concept of freedom of choice is properly understood, we can resolve the issue of the role of reason in freedom of choice. The resolution requires that we understand a subtle point. When we exercise freedom of choice governed by reason, we *also* exercise freedom of choice to be so governed.

This raises the question, however, of which comes first in explanation: the choice to be governed by reason, or the governance of reason in the choice. Does the freedom of choice to be governed by reason come first and explain the role of reason? That would make the role of reason secondary to choice in an account of freedom of choice. Or, on the other hand, does the governance of reason in choice come first and explain our freedom of choice? That would allow that choice bound by reason could explain freedom of choice. How are we to explain the role of reason in freedom of choice without the paradox that reason must be secondary in freedom of choice or become dominant and undermine freedom? To answer the question, we shall need to employ the conception of ultimate preference formulated in the first chapter.

Internal Freedom of Choice: Beyond Desire

Remember our distinction of first-order desire and higher-order preference. Harry G. Frankfurt (1971, 1988) argued very plausibly that we have free will when we do what we desire, with the proviso that we have higher-level desires that endorse our first-level desire. It must be conceded to such a position that a person will claim that he is acting of his own free will when he does what he desires and, moreover, when he desires to have the desire in question. If the matter is left without further comment or qualification, doubts easily arise, as Frankfurt (1988) noted. However, suppose a person, Desiresit, such that the person's desire, and even the desire for the desire, are not subject to the supervision of reason. Whatever the person Desiresit desires, looking inward as he desires to desire, and, looking outward, he does. We further imagine that the person just automatically desires to desire what he desires without reflection or the intervention of rational processes. Given ordinary conflict between desires, this may appear unrealistic, but it is not difficult to imagine a person so constructed internally that his desires, though they might conflict, are automatically put in order. Desiresit does what he desires and desires to desire. He will feel as though he is acting of his free will.

Would we agree that Desiresit has freedom of choice? When we reflect that harmony between first- and second-level desires may arise automatically by an internal mechanism of which the agent may be innocent, it appears that the answer is negative. It might not be up to an agent that she chooses what she desires or that the higher-level desire automatically accords with her first-level desire. The desires favor the choice and the act at all levels, but it is not up to the agent that she responds in accord with her desires in what she does at the first or second level. Desire does not seem sufficient to express freedom of choice, whether a desire is a first- or higher-level desire, because desires may elicit response in us quite automatically and in a way that is indifferent to our approval or rational evaluation. The appropriate state to express freedom of choice should be one that we prefer to so choose, that is up to us. It should not be automatic response to a state like desire, which in many instances, perhaps most typically, elicits response in us without our rational approval or consent. This is what motivates the idea that freedom of choice should be the expression of rational processes, or at least be subject to the supervision of rational processes, as Fischer (1994) has argued. There is nothing in desire, whether at the first or second or next level, to ensure that the agent responding to the desires is capable of effective evaluation of the desire, or capable of being guided by rational processes in choice. Freedom of choice may be entirely lacking.

Moreover, a person sometimes chooses to do something that the person has no desire to do. As I contemplate filling out my tax form, I am as certain as I am about any aspect of my psychology that I have no desire to fill out my tax form. I do not think that I am at all unusual in this respect. Someone might object that I might have a desire to avoid the consequences of not completing the form, and about this they would be right. But that is not the ultimate explanation of my choice. I am convinced of the importance of taxation. I am convinced of the utility of it. I vote against candidates who would lower or eliminate taxes. I am convinced, as a result of reflecting on the appropriate role of government, of the importance of taxation in a democratic society. My approval, indeed, my moral approval of taxation, does not produce a desire for it, however. In terms of desire, I am like everyone else who pays taxes desiring not to do so. I may prefer to choose to do something, like paying my taxes, I do not desire to do.

Rational reflection leads me to accept my views about taxation. When I pay my taxes and fill out the tax form to pay my taxes, I am following the directive of my rational consideration. Yet I still have no desire whatever to subject myself to the very unpleasant task of filling out the form or, for that matter, writing a check and parting with my money. It is just that I am convinced that this is what I ought to do. I simply do not have a desire to do what I am convinced I ought to do. I choose to do what I think I ought to do because of reasons that I have for thinking that I ought to do it. I do not need desire nudging me to do what I think that I ought to do. Contrary to David Hume, reason need not always serve the passions. It has other business. I do not have to wait for a desire to arise in me to drive my sense of obligation to choose and act. It is up to me whether I go where reason and obligation direct. I do not, having reflected on what I ought to do and having reached a conclusion, sit by helplessly waiting for some desire to make me choose to act. It is up to me, whether I like or dread this, and I am the author of my choice as I exercise my own freedom of choice.

Preference and Metamental Ascent

Still, one like me might ask, "Isn't there some disposition, perhaps not desire, that leads me to choose what I am convinced I ought to do?" Am I not disposed to do what I am convinced by reason that I ought to do? The answer is affirmative. I prefer to do what I am convinced I ought to do, even though I do not desire to do what I am convinced I ought to do. People sometimes prefer to do what they desire, but not always, as the example of filling out tax forms illustrates. But even in the tax case there is a difference between higher-order preference and first-order desire, as noted in the previous chapter. I may prefer to satisfy a desire or prefer not to satisfy the desire, or I may prefer to ignore a desire and do what I consider to be rational or obligatory without desire to do so. It is crucial to attend to the distinction between preference and desire. My theory of the matter, which I have articulated in some detail elsewhere (Lehrer 1990a, 1997a), is that a philosophically satisfactory theory of the mind will distinguish between a first-order state of desire and a higher-order state of preference, which differs from desire because preference is a preference over alternatives, including even higher-order desires. The choice of the words "desire" and "preference" seems appropriate to my theoretical usage, but I acknowledge that neither ordinary nor philosophical usage is consistent on this linguistic point. My usage is, in part, stipulative.

It should be noted that this metamental ascent to evaluation and preference is a feature of our mental and metamental capacities. I am not arguing that it is impossible to resolve conflict without metamental ascent. I am claiming, on the basis of observation, that we do it this way. We are able to place our desires before the higher-order bar of judgment and evaluate their merits. Moreover, such a perspective often enables us to see how to resolve conflict and even maximize the satisfaction of desires. The evaluation of desires enters into this process if we are moral and rational. Some desires are immoral and others irrational, but some are also appropriate, so reflection on how to satisfy our desires typically presupposes evaluation of desires and the formation of preferences concerning which ones, if any, to satisfy.

It is possible, however, to imagine a logically possible creature who is incapable of metamental ascent but who has exactly the same dispositions to choose as we possess. What is the advantage of metamental ascent and higher-order evaluation? The process is heuristic and provides for our plasticity, our ability to change, to change our principles, and even to change how we change. We might have been made as first-order creatures with unreflective principles and dispositions for conflict resolution. But then we would lack the plasticity to change our principles of choice because we would be ignorant of them, and, therefore, we could not know them clearly enough to override them. Given our metamental capacity, we can both evaluate how to choose and how to change how we choose. The claim that we choose by evaluating our desires is supported by observation and explained by the heuristic of metamental plasticity, that is, plasticity resulting from our higher-order mental life. Our freedom of choice depends on this metamental capacity and the plasticity of our mental life.

Of course, preference may also be principled to guide choice. One use of principle, and an important one, is to have a rule of thumb for the satisfaction of desires in order to provide for an economy of effort. We do not need to reflect on the question of whether to satisfy each desire that arises because some desires are innocuous. Such desires may be satisfied without deliberation in ordinary circumstances, for example, drinking a glass of water from the tap when one is thirsty and has a desire to drink. The satisfaction of such a desire without thinking about whether to satisfy it or not in ordinary circumstances is neither irrational nor immoral.

Some unreflective behavior is no doubt spontaneous, but we should not assume that the preference to satisfy desires without reflecting upon them is entirely controlled at the first level. The higher-order certification of some desires in ordinary circumstances remains. It may be authorized by preference sufficient for freedom of choice because it is under the active power and influence of the metamind. The rule or principle to satisfy such desires without deliberation is a rule of thumb that is defeasible and may be overridden. The role of the rule is rather like an intention to satisfy such desires, as Michael E. Bratman (1987) analyzes intention. An intention, as he analyzes it, may direct choice without reflection but is open to reconsideration and, indeed, alteration. To convince oneself of this, consider the way in which we unreflectively satisfy the desire to open mail that is addressed to us until circumstances change and raise our suspicions about whether our mail might be contaminated by poison and whether there could be danger in following the usual rule of thumb. We then see that the rule or principle that embodied our preference is not an automatic first-order operation, but it is an intention to follow a rule under metamental supervision and is subject to reconsideration and revision.

Preference and Power Preference

There has been much controversy about whether a person whose first- and second-order desires are in accord therefore acts freely in the satisfaction of the first-order desire. The question is whether such accord among our desires is sufficient for freedom of choice. We have seen argument that it is not. Some external influence might have the power to automatically align such desires beyond the control of the agent. Moreover, just as accord among our desires is not sufficient for preference that yields freedom of choice, it is not necessary either. Conflict among desires is compatible with preference expressed in freedom of choice. We may be acutely aware of our freedom of choice when we have a conflict between our desires. For then we are forced to reflect upon our desires and form a preference for the satisfaction of some but not all of our desires, or, perhaps, for none of them. Moreover, the conflict among desires may be a conflict among desires at different levels. I might have a first-level desire to eat some rich food laden with butter. I might have a second-level desire not to have such a desire because of a concern for the effect of butter on my arteries. I might even have a third-order desire to be a rugged character who was not so concerned about his health. And so forth. I might be rife with conflicting desires that articulate themselves at different levels without my preference or freedom of choice being infringed upon in a significant way. Indeed, I may take some pleasure in looking upon all these unruly desires and putting them in some order to form a preference about whether to satisfy the desire to eat the buttery food on this occasion. Imagine I reflect as follows: it is up to me and in my power to determine which of these desires I shall prefer to satisfy. I might find this reflection to be a source of satisfaction, seeing myself as empowered to choose, or a source of anxiety, seeing myself as responsible for the choice. Which desires, if any, I evaluate positively and prefer to satisfy is up to me, when I have power of preference sufficient for freedom of choice.

Having noted that freedom of choice pertains to preference rather than desire, the question immediately arises as to what is required for a preference to sustain the power of freedom of choice against influences that might otherwise dominate preference. To return to our initial problem, might not reason influence what we prefer? If it does, how can we say that it is preference and not reason that determines the choice? Should we say that it is the nature of preference to provide freedom of choice? Are higher-order evaluation and the formation of preference sufficient for freedom of choice? The usual objection is that preference, even if metamental, does not provide us with a secure prophylactic against manipulation by a variety of external and internal influences that might dominate preference. Indeed, the objection might proceed, higher-order metamental ascent merely provides us with greater cognitive advantages. As a result of metamental ascent, we might know what we desire and what the merits and demerits of satisfying a desire are, but such information, though it might insure us against some forms of ignorance about our desires, does not insure us against some forms of manipulation and control. Our metamental evaluations and resulting preferences might themselves be under the control of another agent. How we evaluate and what we prefer might be in his power, not ours. In this case, our preferences, no matter how rational and moral they might appear to us, could be the result of the power that another has over us rather than an exercise of our freedom of choice. The higher-order ascent to preference is not sufficient to ensure freedom of choice.

What must we add to preferences to ensure that? Will higher-order preferences or counterfactual conditions concerning preferences provide the needed prophylactic? Suppose, for example, that moving from the inflexibility of desire to the plasticity of preference, we consider whether a higher-order preference for a lower level of preference suffices for freedom of choice of the lower-level preference. It is clear from our considerations of higher-order desires that this higher-order preference for a lower preference does not suffice for the freedom of choice of the latter. The entire preference structure, from the lowest- to the highest-level preference, might be in the control of another agent and be manipulated by this other agent.

Consider, then, the addition of counterfactual conditions, ones to the effect that if I had preferred to have other preferences than I do, then I would have had other preferences. Thus, for example, suppose that if I had preferred at the second level not to have my preference to make a painting of Finger Rock Canyon, then I would not have had my first-order preference to paint it, even though, in fact, I have a first-order preference to paint it. Does this ensure, as G. E. Moore (1912) once suggested concerning choice, that I am free or have free will? Unfortunately, it does not, and the objection is familiar from the discussion concerning Moore and his followers. The second-order preference might not be in my control. That preference also may be manipulated by another agent. Thus, even if my first-order preference would have been different if my second-order preference had been different, this does not ensure that I am free in the first-order preference. I might not be free in the second-order preference. The latter might not be under my control.

In an earlier attempt to meet this objection (Lehrer 1980, 1990b), I suggested iterating the counterfactual condition and requiring that if I had preferred at any level to have a different preference at the next lower level, then I would have had a different preference at the next lower level. My purpose was to ensure that I had an answer to the question of whether my preference at any level is in my power. My answer to the question of whether the preference at some specified level is in my power would be that if I had preferred to prefer otherwise at the specified level, then I would have preferred otherwise at that level. Is this counterfactual condition sufficient for the preference being in my power? Again, there is a difficulty concerning control raised by Peter Van Inwagen (1983) and Krister Segerberg (1983). It is that the sequence of higher-order preferences and the counterfactual conditions concerning preferences might be in the control of another agent. Imagine that what I do prefer and what I would prefer if I had preferred to prefer otherwise are completely controlled by another. To get specific about the control, suppose that a small computer chip was secretly installed in my brain. Call it, as I have, a "braino," which enables an external operator to determine what preferences I have. In fact, all of my preferences are controlled by the operator. It might then be true that if I had preferred to have other preferences, I would have had other preferences, but this is because the operator with the braino would have determined that I had other preferences. It is not my freedom of choice but his control of the braino that determines what preference I have and, moreover, would have at each level.

Agency and Active Power

To capture the notion of freedom of choice, something else is required than just preference, something else than just next-level preferences over a preference of a given level, and something more than counterfactual influence of preferences over preferences. But what? Someone might be inclined to give up the quest for explanation at this point and just answer, "freedom of choice." A philosopher should not give up the quest for explanation, however, until there is proof that none can be given. One further attempt at explanation is to appeal to a notion of agency or agent causality. Thomas Reid (1895) suggests that liberty requires that I determine my volitions, which include my preferences. Reid uses the notion of "liberty" as implying "freedom of choice," so Reid would claim that to be free in my preferences, I must be the cause of them. Others, most notably Richard Taylor (1966) and Roderick M. Chisholm (1966), have reintroduced this doctrine into discussion in the latter part of the twentieth century. Some have found the notion of agent causality to be unintelligible, but Reid (1895) argues that this is the primary notion of causality, though unanalyzable. Other notions of causality, Reid alleges, are but metaphorical extensions of it. So to ensure the presence of freedom of choice and to avoid the problem of manipulation, Reid might just have added that the free agent must be the cause of his or her preferences. Should we settle for this solution?

Seeking to explain as much as we can and to leave as little unexplained as we must, we need to ask whether we can analyze this notion of agent causality. I suggest that we need not take the notion as primitive, but that we can explain it. So let us take a few further steps toward explanation. First of all, let us make explicit the notion of a preference structure concerning some action A. By this I shall mean a first-order preference concerning action A and other, higher-order preferences pertaining to action A. One simple example of a preference structure would be a preference to paint Finger Rock Canyon, a second-order preference to have this first-order preference, and a third-order preference to have the second-order preference, and so on up the orders of preference as far as they extend. This is an integrated structure of level-specific preference without conflict. However, free preference, which we shall later define in terms of a power preference as we did in earlier chapters, may be based on a preference structure that contains conflict. Moreover, the higher-order preferences need not be stratified by levels, that is, they need not be level specific. For example, a preference concerning all of my preferences pertaining to action A would not be level specific.

Moreover, free preference need not depend on an infinite hierarchy of preferences, though an infinite hierarchy of preferences is possible. We can suppose that a person has an infinite hierarchy, especially an integrated one, since preferences are functional states, not occurrent states. A functional state, like a dispositional state, is a standing state having a certain role to function in a determinate manner in thought, reasoning, and choice. Moreover, since preferences are functional states, there is no need to suppose that they can be understood in a momentary intuition. The understanding of them may itself be computational or functional. In the simple example considered above, there is no difficulty with computing higher-order preferences from lower-level ones or, for that matter, lower-level preferences from higher-order ones. The computational rule says this: to go up a preference level, just add a preference to the last preference considered, and to go down a preference level, just delete the last preference from the last preference considered. However, an infinite hierarchy of preferences is neither sufficient for freedom of choice, as we noted above, nor necessary, for reasons that we shall now consider.

A preference may be level-ambiguous and incorporate conflict. Suppose, for example, that I consider all preferences that I have concerning an action A and find that, whatever conflicts or other peculiarities I discern, I am satisfied with the preference structure just as it is. I evaluate it positively. Thus, I prefer to have this preference structure, including all of my preferences pertaining to action A—to writing this essay, for example. I might prefer to have this preference. Indeed, I do. This is not without conflict, but all things considered, I prefer to have all the preferences that I do concerning writing this essay. Notice, however, that this very preference to have the preferences that I do concerning writing this essay is, itself, a preference concerning writing this essay. So this preference, being a preference for having the preference structure containing all my preferences concerning writing the essay, is contained in the preference structure because it is also a preference concerning writing this essay. This preference for the preference structure is not level specific. This preference for the preference structure is a preference for the preferences within the preference structure.

I have in previous chapters called this preference for the preference structure, or more personally, my preference for my preference structure to do A, my *power preference* concerning A. I shall argue that such a preference empowers me and is the basis of my freedom of choice. A philosopher who is determined to stratify preferences by levels might suppose that it would be possible to assign the power preference a higher level than any of the preferences in the preference structure. It is a preference "over" the preferences in the preference structure. This attempt to assign a level to the power preference, in addition to being a deviant notion of "level," would be a mistake, however. The reason noted above is that the power preference is itself a preference in the preference structure pertaining to A. The power preference is a preference concerning preferences pertaining to action A. Thus, my power preference for the preference structure loops back onto itself in the preference structure. It is a preference for all of the preferences in the preference structure, including itself. This is the secret source of the power of the power preference.

The loop of the power preference back onto itself in the preference structure is a special feature of the freedom of choice. Consider my preference for A. Now suppose that a question arises as to the freedom of choice of the preference. I might try to assure myself or another agent that the preference suffices for freedom by appealing to a preference for that preference. But this will leave the question of the freedom of choice of that next-level preference unanswered. One might, of course, argue that the first preference to do A suffices for freedom because of the second preference for the first, even if the second preference is not free. This would leave us with the need to explain how a second preference that is not free could be sufficient to ensure the freedom of choice of the first preference. One might just insist that it is sufficient without explanation, but that would leave us with an unexplained "surd," and one seeking, as I do, to explain as much as possible, will not be satisfied with a "surd."

To avoid the "surd," one might embrace a regress and add a third preference for the second, a fourth for the third, to answer the question of whether the first preference is free. So one might embrace a regress of explanations to avoid the "surd." The infinite regress, though it is not vicious because preferences are functional states, is not satisfying either. For it leaves open the question of whether the infinite sequence is free. By contrast, the power preference answers all questions about preferences concerning preferences pertaining to A in a single preference, the preference for the preference structure. Since this preference loops back onto itself as a preference in the preference structure, the preference contains within itself a preference for itself and avoids the "surd" and the regress. The question whether it is preferred is answered by the preference itself without need to appeal to another preference. It is preferred in a way that is sufficient to ensure that it and all the other preferences in the preference structure are preferences that the agent prefers to have. A power preference ties the preferences in the preference structure up, down, and together in a loop of preference that empowers us.

Ungrounded Preference and Freedom

Is the power preference sufficient to ensure freedom of choice? It frees preference of external semantic constraints because of the self-referential feature of it. In this way it is like the claim "All true sentences are true," which says of other true sentences that they are true and, at the same time, if it is true, says of itself that it is true. In a similar way the power preferences—my preference to have the preference structure that I do have pertaining to choosing action A—is a preference for all the other preferences that I have pertaining to the choice, and, at the same time, it is a preference for having the power preference itself. The truth of having the preference is internal to preference without external semantic grounding.

Such semantic ungroundedness, discussed by Saul Kripke (1975), might be considered a semantic defect, but, as Vann McGee (1991) has shown, *the ungroundedness of a sentence does not mean that it lacks a truth-value*. Rather, the ungroundedness means that the truth-value is a matter of choice. Consider again the sentence, "All true sentences are true." This sentence, if true, says of itself, as well as other sentences, something that might be expressed by the sentence "This sentence is true." The truth of this latter sentence, if it is true, is not grounded in any antecedently specified truth conditions. Let us say, therefore, that this latter sentence is "ungrounded." We can choose to assign it a truth-value: for example, we can choose to assign it the value "true," but this choice will not be grounded in any externally specified truth conditions. So the ungroundedness of the power preference does not mean that there is no truth-value to the claim that such a power preference exists, but only that the truth-value depends on choice. The ungroundedness provides a kind of semantic independence, therefore, which is a virtue of the power preference as a condition of freedom of choice. *We want the freedom of choice of our preference to depend on our preference itself. Power preference is the surrogate of free choice.*

The internal structure and, indeed, the semantic structure of the power preference reveals its merit for the role of explicating freedom of choice. However, this does not mean that the power preference is a sufficient condition for freedom. There are two reasons for this. The first concerns the possibility of external manipulation. The second concerns the possibility of internal compulsion. Consideration of both will take us back to the paradox of reason with which we began. Consider the possibility of external manipulation. A power preference, though semantically ungrounded, may result from choice, and choice may be externally controlled. Another person might direct my thoughts and preferences for choice. We can imagine a braino installed in my brain, as we did above, that is controlled by another person who operates the braino to cause me to form my preferences, including a preference for having the preference structure that I have. The braino might be used to cause my power preference. Without electronic control of my brain, another person might make use of psychological compulsion. If another person knows that a certain line of reasoning, perhaps one that appeals to religious authority, will make me choose to prefer a course of action and to have a power preference for the preference structure pertaining to this choice of action, then I am subject to manipulation by the other person in my power preference by a line of reasoning of religious authority.

It is clear that such manipulative causation of the power preference deprives me of freedom of choice, however satisfied I might be with the power preference. My preference for the preference structure that I have, including this power preference itself, might be controlled by another person. Should we conclude from this that a power preference must be uncaused, as libertarians might propose, to ensure that the preference suffices for freedom? This proposal might appear promising as a solution to the problem, until we remember that we need some positive account of how a person can be the cause of his or her preferences. The mere fact that a preference of mine is uncaused, even a power preference, does not ensure that the preference is up to me or that I am the cause of it. In short, the denial of external causal etiology of a power preference leaves us without a positive account of a relationship of an agent to a power preference to ensure that it suffices for freedom. Are we caught in a dilemma then? Must we say that if my preference, even a power preference, is caused, then it does not suffice for freedom because it is caused, and if it is uncaused, then here, too, it is not sufficient because I am not the cause of my preference? Is there any explanation of how I can be the cause of a preference, including my power preference, that precludes control of my preferences by another or by some compulsion?

Ultimate Preference and the Primacy Condition

The answer is contained in our earlier formulation of a power preference that is the primary explanation of choice, in the terminology of the previous chapter an ultimate preference. We must require that the power preference be a preference that a person has because he or she prefers to have that preference. We need to add that the person has the power preference that he or she has because he or she prefers to have it in a rather special way explained in chapter 2. Most simply put, the power preference must be the primary explanation for why he or she has the power preference. The power preference on the part of the agent, which is self-explanatory, as we have noted, must be the primary and ultimate explanation of the existence of the power preference. The power preference is a preference concerning a specific choice, and it is also a preference for itself. If one asks why the person has the power preference, the answer is that he has it because he prefers to have it, albeit, in a primary explanatory way. There may be many components to a complete explanation of a preference, but for the power preference to suffice for freedom, the power preference must be the primary explanation for itself. That means that it is an ultimate explanation essential and adequate without appeal to other explanatory conditions. This condition will be called here *the primacy condition*. If the power preference is manipulated by another to yield the choice, the power preference is not the primary explanation, not an ultimate explanation. Why is it not primary in the case of manipulation? In that case manipulation of the power preference is essential to an adequate explanation. The power preference is not an ultimate explanation.

Agent Causality Explained

Let us note the advantages of this account and then return to the paradox of reason. First of all, a power preference that satisfies the primacy condition offers us an explanation of agent causality. Such a preference is one that I have because I am the cause of the preference. Why? If I have a preference *because* I prefer to have it, then I, not someone else, am the cause of the preference. Consider again the case of the braino. In that case, the operator of the braino, not I, is the cause of my preferences, even my power preferences. In such a case, I do not have a preference because I prefer to have it.

I have it because the braino operator prefers that I have it. I have the preferences that I do because he operates the machine rather than because I prefer to have them. The primacy condition requiring that the preference be the ultimate explanation of choice is not satisfied. The explanation of why I have the power preference is that the machine operator causes it, not that I do. The primacy condition is not satisfied. Alternatively, if the primacy condition is satisfied, and I have the power preference because I prefer to have it as the ultimate preference of the choice, then the preference is not controlled by the operator of the braino. If he controlled it, then I would not have the preference because I preferred to have it but because he preferred that I have it. When the primacy condition explains why I am the cause of the power preference, why it is an ultimate preference, then I have that preference *because* I prefer to have it.

This account of agent causality avoids the regress and "surd." There is no regress because the power preference loops back onto itself and is a preference for itself as well as for other preferences pertaining to the action A. There is no "surd" because there is no appeal to a self that causes a preference in some unexplained or mysterious way. On the contrary, the explanation for the preference is a preference, and causation of preferences by preferences is not mysterious. The looping character of the preference might seem to introduce something odd if not mysterious. Isn't the idea of a preference existing because it is a preference for itself a mysterious one? The answer, which will be elaborated upon further when we consider the solution to the paradox of reason, is that components in a structure can be mutually supporting in ordinary causal terms. Consider a keystone in the structure of an arch constructed Andy Goldsworthy style without cement or artificial attachment of the stones. They just lean against each other to form an arch. This kind of mutual causal support sustaining an arch, though a work of art, is not causally mysterious. It is gravity artistically exploited. My claim is that the structure of preferences causally resembles this physical structure. The power preference playing the role of the keystone as a metaphor or model for a keystone in the structure of preferences may be causally supported by the other preferences in the structure at the same time that it causally supports the structure and itself within the structure.

Power Preference and Preference of Others

The metaphor of an arch containing a keystone calls our attention to the need for considering the position of the power preference in satisfying the primacy condition in the broader "structure" of causes. First of all, consider the causal influence of the preferences of another agent. We appear to obtain a paradoxical result if we concede that we sometimes have the preferences that we do because of the preferences of others. Can we freely prefer and choose to satisfy the preferences of another? Is that freedom of choice? How can I have the preferences that I do pertaining to choosing an action because I prefer to have them, if I choose what I do because you prefer that I choose in that way? This paradox concerning the influence of preferences of others is similar to the paradox of reason with which we began. How can I have the preferences that I do pertaining to a choice of an action because I prefer to have them if I have the preferences that I do because of the *reasons* that I have for these preferences?

Let us consider the paradox concerning the preferences of others. The solution to it rests on drawing a distinction between different ways in which I can be influenced by the preferences of another person. At one extreme, there is the control of my preferences in some concealed way by another so that I do not even perceive that I am controlled at all. A bit less extreme is the case in which I prefer what I do because of my knowledge of the preferences of another person whom I have a compulsive desire or impulse to satisfy. Extreme cases of obsession with another person, whether as the result of my obsessive love or the other's charismatic power, may have the result that I cannot help preferring what I perceive the other to prefer. It is not just that I desire to do what the other prefers. It is rather that the other has an influence over me of such a systematic sort that it extends beyond my first-order desire to higher-level evaluation and preference. Obsessive love or charismatic power may have this feature. In these states, my mind and metamind are taken over by the other, so that whatever the other values, I have to value, and whatever the other prefers, I have to prefer. There is no freedom of choice here.

How can I freely prefer what the other prefers? Imagine I prefer to satisfy the preferences of the other because I have a power preference to prefer to have such preferences. If the power preference is an ultimate preference I have because I prefer to have it, then I am free. On the contrary, if I prefer to satisfy the preferences of the other but I do not have that preference because I prefer to have it, I may be enslaved to the other. In short, whether I am free depends on whether the preference that I have for satisfying the preferences of the other results from a power preference that satisfies the primacy condition and is an ultimate preference of mine. If I have the power preference because I prefer to have it, if that is my ultimate preference, then I am free. If not, I may be in bondage to the powers of the other. To be free, I must have the power preference to satisfy the preferences of the other because I prefer to have the power preference for the preferences of the other. My power preference for my preference structure must be the ultimate explanation for the choice, one that stands alone without appeal to other conditions to explain my choice.

The Paradox of Reason Solved

These reflections on the paradox concerning the preferences of others lead to the solution of the paradox of reason. How can I have the preferences that I do because I prefer to have them if I have these preferences because of the reasons that I have for having them? The answer is more complicated than the explanation of how we can freely prefer to satisfy the preferences of another person, but the fundamental idea is the same. I can be enslaved by reasons just as I can be enslaved by the preferences of another. But preferring something because of the reasons that I have for preferring it, like preferring something because of the preferences of another, need not be bondage that destroys freedom of choice. If my response to reasons like my response to the preferences of another finds a primary explanation in my power preferences, then the response may be free in spite of the causal influences. Another person could have such amorous or charismatic power over me as to supply me with reasons that become my reasons for forming a preference because of his or her power over me. If I cannot resist the other person, then my power preference does not suffice for freedom of choice. It does not matter whether the reasons are good reasons or bad ones. If I respond to them because of the power of the other, if the power of the other is the primary explanation of why I form my preference in accord with these reasons, then my preferences do not suffice for freedom of choice.

Reason and Freedom of Choice

I may, however, form a preference in accord with reasons in a way that is compatible with freedom of choice. The way should now be clear. First of all, I must form a preference in accord with reasons because I prefer to do so. Second, this preference accords with a power preference for the preference satisfying the primacy condition. Therefore, this is an ultimate explanation for my preference. I am free in preferring what I choose to do for the reasons that I have under what I call an *ultimate preference* when the power preference for my so choosing is the ultimate explanation for my choosing in accord with those reasons. It might seem that this solution to the paradox of reason only calls up another paradox, however. For now, it seems that I can only form preferences in accord with reasons that suffice for freedom of choice if I first prefer proceeding in accord with the reasons. This naturally raises the question of whether these preferences for forming preferences in accord with reasons are themselves be formed in accord with reasons. It appears, therefore, that we might be forced to concede that some preferences that suffice for freedom of choice cannot be formed in accord with reasons. Consider a difficult choice. A philosopher, Anne, is trying to decide whether to change her career in a major way, like Luce in chapter 1. As she remarks on the difficulty of the choice, we advise her that, since she is a philosopher, all she needs to do is tally up her reasons and choose. She may justly reply, like Luce, that we do not understand the seriousness of the matter, for she first has to decide which reasons are to guide her choice. Must we agree that this decision is one she must make without appeal to reasons?

Not at all. Her decision may be surrounded with reasons. It must be conceded that it is important for Anne to reflect on the reasons that she already has as she decides what reasons she prefers to guide her choice. In fact, however, the choice of what career she will prefer, and the choice of what reasons will determine her preference, may well occur together. When she has a preference for forming her career preference in accord with some reasons and not others, she may, at the same time, form her preference for choice in accord with those reasons. In fact, the decision to prefer one career over another and the decision to form her preferences in accord with some reasons over others may coincide functionally as well as temporally. Her preference to pursue a career that she finds personally rewarding may be functionally equivalent to preferring to be guided by reasoning to prefer her career. She finds the career personally rewarding. Which comes first, the career preference, or the preference to be guided by the reasons that support this career preference? This question is answered by denying that one has to come before the other. The career preference and the preference to be guided by reasons that support this career preference may occur at the same time and be mutually supportive.

A critic may persist and claim that even if they occur at the same time, one must be the cause or explanation of the other and, therefore, have causal or explanatory precedence or dominance over the other. The reply is that her career preference and her preference to form such preferences by reasons may be mutually supportive in the way that two cards leaning against each other are mutually supportive—or, to take my favorite metaphor, in the way that stones in an arch support the keystone as It supports them, so that the structure remains standing because of a loop of mutual support. Suppose, too, that the critic of my theory is moved to protest that even if the career preference and the preference to be guided by reasons that support the career preference are simultaneous and mutually supportive, there is a problem about the freedom of choice of the preference to be guided by reasons that support the career preference. What would make this choice free? The answer, of course, is that the preference must be a preference that the person has because she prefers the preference structure concerning that preference. That is, there is a power preference satisfying the primacy condition that is an ultimate explanation for that preference. It is, therefore, an ultimate preference and that suffices for free choice.

Can the formation of preference for some special reason, because it satisfies the categorical imperative, for example, suffice for freedom of choice without the satisfaction of the primacy condition? To test this idea, consider a philosopher, similar to Kant (1959), who forms a preference to tell the truth and not to lie, for the reason that it satisfies the categorical imperative. Is this sufficient for the person to be free in choosing to tell the truth? Suppose that another person, Pseudokant, forms his preferences for the reason that they satisfy the categorical imperative, but Pseudokant is a victim of a braino implanted in his brain, which allows the operator, Controller, to determine what reasons will move Pseudokant to form his preferences. Controller chooses to force Pseudokant be guided by the categorical imperative in his formation of preferences.

Pseudokant is not free, no matter how perfectly he is guided by the categorical imperative, because he is controlled by another person in how he forms his preferences, as I am confident Kant would agree. The problem for Pseudokant is not that he fails to form his preferences on the basis of the categorical imperative, but that his formation of preferences on the basis of the categorical imperative, even if he prefers to form preferences in this way, is the result of the intervention of Controller. Pseudokant does not form preferences because he prefers to form preferences on the basis of the categorical imperative, but because Controller makes him form his preferences in this way. Notice that even if Controller creates a preference in Pseudokant for forming preferences in a way that satisfies the categorical imperative, Pseudokant will not have this preference as an ultimate preference. In short, he will lack a power preference satisfying the primacy condition for an ultimate preference for forming his preferences in the way that he does. Freedom of choice supplements rationality rather than being a consequence of it.

Reason and Freedom of Choice: The Ultrapreference

Some contemporary authors, among them John Martin Fischer (1994) and J. David Velleman (1992), have tried to reduce freedom or freedom of choice to the influence and governance of reasons in preference and choice. But any such account will fall short unless it somehow guarantees that a person is free in the way in which the person is influenced by or governed by reasons. The influence and governance by reasons, no matter how admirably rational, can be controlled by another person. The result is that the controlled individual lacks freedom of choice. We must add freedom of choice to any account of being influenced or governed by reasons, rather than expect that freedom of choice should be a consequence of such influence or governance. The preference to be guided or governed by a system of reasons, SR, in forming a preference, P, must be free in order for the preference P, guided by reasons, to be free. Does this preference to be so guided or governed lead us to a regress of preferences?

It does not. Call the preference to be guided or governed by a system of reasons an *ultrapreference*. Now suppose that there is a power preference satisfying the primacy condition for the ultrapreference. This power preference may have many features of any other preference. It may be a preference in a preference structure, and the person may prefer to have this structure because the person prefers to have it. In short, there may be a power preference for the preference structure containing the ultrapreference. The looping character of the power preference again avoids the regress and the "surd." Must the ultrapreference be a preference that a person forms, as Sartre (1956) suggests, without justification and without excuse?[1] Not at all. The ultrapreference may be a preference that the person forms guided or governed by the system of reasons, SR. The ultrapreference is governed by the system of reasons, SR, at the same time that the ultrapreference is a preference to be governed by SR, and so there is a loop of preference back on to itself. This loop of preference, which may include the power preference for the governance by the system of reasons, SR, is the loop of freedom of choice that ties freedom of choice and rationality together.

---

[1] I was not able to link this interpretation to a specific passage, for his prose has a charmingly diffuse character, but I am indebted to Jean-Paul Sartre (1956), *Being and Nothingness*.

A Summary on Preferences, Reason, and Freedom of Choice

Let us retrace our path and end with a consideration of the perennial problem of freedom and determinism, reinterpreted as the problem of freedom of choice and determinism. We began by asking how we might solve the paradox of reason: that is, if we are governed by reasons in our preferences, then we are in bondage to reason and not free, whereas if we are not governed by reason, then we lack reasons for our free choices. We noted that the solution is that we may have an ultimate power preference to be guided by reasons in forming our preferences. Moreover, this ultimate preference itself may be guided by the reasons that we prefer to guide us. This becomes possible once one notes that ultimate preference contains a power preference for one's preference structure. This power preference is itself a preference in the preference structure and, therefore, loops back onto itself. The result is that the ultimate preference is a power preference satisfying the primacy condition. I am the cause of it. I have the power preference because I prefer to have it. No regress results from this account of freedom of choice. Finally, we are not left with some "surd" of an unexplained or unjustified preference. The ultimate preference is self-explained by the fact that I have it because I prefer to have it and for the reasons that I prefer to govern my preferences.

Arational Freedom of Choice, Causation, and Determinism

We are left with two perennial problems that we are now in a position to answer. The first concerns whether we must be governed by reasons in order to be free. The view of freedom of choice advanced in this chapter is compatible with arationalism. Suppose that a person prefers at time t not to be guided by reasons in the future.

He may even have reasons for this at time t. Moreover, his choice for not being guided by reasons in the future may be free. Consider any time later than t. At such a time, the person may prefer what he does without being guided by reasons at that time. He might not even be guided by the reasons that he had at t for preferring not to be guided by reasons in the future. The future that was referred to at t is now present, and he might not be guided by any reasons, including the earlier ones, in his present preferences and choices. His present preferences may, nonetheless, be preferences in a preference structure that he has because he prefers to have it. He has become arationally free. Freedom of choice supplements rationality as we exercise freedom of choice when we choose to be guided by a system of reasons, or, equally, when we choose not to be so guided. When we are guided by a system of reasons, we direct our attention to our higher-order system. By contrast, when we turn away from being guided by reasons, whether generally in the extreme choice of arationality, or in some specific instance requiring fast response, we often turn our attention to first-order response. In specific cases, like driving a car under busy conditions, attending in the mode of first-order response rather than pondering some higher-order path of reason, might save fenders.

The second problem is whether the account of freedom of choice that I have proposed is logically consistent with causal determinism. The answer will, of course, depend on how one defines determinism, and I shall examine the definitions in the next chapter. The simplest answer, however, is that free choice is logically consistent with the power preference explaining the choice itself being causally explained. Moreover, the conditions of causal explanation may extend in a sequence as far back in time as one cares to imagine. All that is required for freedom of choice is that the primary explanation for the power preference for the choice of A at time t, is that the person has the preference at time t because he or she prefers to have it at time t. That explanation must be an ultimate explanation that is essential and adequate to explain the choice at time t.

The power preference stands alone as an explanation of itself. There might be some secondary explanation, and further explanation beyond that, and so forth back into the indefinite past. One might object that remote explanations, no matter how secondary, are causal conditions over which the person had no control. The answer is that there are always causal conditions of our preferences over which we had no control, for example, our being born. If it is asked whether we could have preferred to choose otherwise at time t, we may answer briefly that we could have, provided that our power preference for choosing otherwise would have been the ultimate explanation for choosing otherwise at time t. This condition is logically consistent with a causal explanation of preference that extends in a secondary way as far back into the past as one cares to imagine, though that explanation is not ultimate.

The burden of the traditional compatibilism, which is the subject of the next chapter, reformed as a condition of logical consistency, is to explain the difference between causation that makes us free in our preferences and causation that puts us in bondage. Here is a précis of the argument to come in the next chapter. The explanation in terms of our power preference for choosing what we do or for choosing otherwise stands alone in an adequate and essential explanatory loop. When we prefer to have the preference structures that we do pertaining to our ultimate preferences because we prefer to have them, we find a place for our freedom of choice in the natural order of things. Freedom of choice and the choices of actions that result from ultimate preferences provide us with the dignity of being free agents in the causal order.

4
Determinism, Ultimate Preference, and the Consistency Claim

This chapter will be my attempt to explain how scientific determinism can be consistent with freedom of choice. The burden is to find a form of preference that explains choice and is logically consistent with scientific determinism. My purpose is to offer an account of freedom of choice that is logically consistent with a scientific theory maintaining that all choice is covered by scientific laws. This could be described as what I called compatibilism, now called *classical* compatibilism, entailing a conception of freedom of choice of an alternative among options, including the minimal option of not choosing what one in fact chooses. Since the term *compatibilism* has been co-opted to involve a weaker constraint on freedom, requiring only that a person do what she fully desires, even if no option is available, I prefer to speak of the *consistency claim*, namely, that freedom of choice containing a choice among options, including the option not to choose as one does, is consistent with scientific laws covering all choice. This chapter is a defense of one form of the consistency claim.

I have discussed the consistency claim in earlier chapters, but my intention here is clarify the logic of the argument. The argument raises two issues immediately. One concerns the meaning of scientific determinism. The other concerns the conception of freedom of choice and how it configures in the logic of the consistency claim. I have already written at length about freedom of choice as the result of explanation by an ultimate preference.

I note here in passing that this form of explanation might be casually rephrased by saying that the ultimate cause of the choice in freedom of choice is the power preference. However, the notion of *cause* is highly contested, most notably since David Hume, and consequently ambiguous. I offered an account of explanation of choice instead of causation in order to avoid ambiguity and clarify the conception of freedom of choice.

A word about the logic of the defense of the consistency claim. The first logical claim to notice is that if there is an explanatory condition, EC, that entails a conception of freedom of choice, FC, and EC, is logically consistent with scientific determinism, SD, then it follows that FC is logically consistent with scientific determinism, SD. Colloquially put, if there is anything that entails freedom of choice that is logically consistent with determinism, then freedom of choice is logically consistent with determinism. Put another way, if there is any condition entailing freedom of choice that does not entail the falsity of determinism, then freedom of choice does not entail the falsity of determinism either. It suffices to establish the consistency claim that ultimate preference both entails freedom of choice and is logically consistent with scientific determinism.

Now, however, the question is what is meant by determinism. The scientific account of determinism is often formulated in terms of nomological deduction. Most simply put, the doctrine is that given a complete description of the state of the universe at any one time, S_x, and a complete list of the scientific laws, L, you can deduce the complete state S_y of the universe at any other time. This is a symmetric version of a deductive nomological account of determinism neglecting the direction of time. An antisymmetric version respecting the direction of time would add the restriction that S_y is later than S_x. The logical implications of this form of determinism for freedom of choice depends on the conception of scientific laws. However, before proceeding to a discussion of scientific laws, I shall present a defense of the consistency claim based on an argument about the logical relation between nomological deduction and explanation.

Nomological Deduction and Explanation

My defense is based on the premise that scientific determinism may fail to explain our choices. Sylvain Bromberger (1965) proved that nomological deduction is not sufficient for explanation. Bromberger (1965, 1993) argued convincingly, and I follow him, that an explanation is an answer to a *why-question* that nomological deduction may fail to answer. An explanation of a person's choice to do A must answer the question, Why did the person choose to do A? There may be many conditions (some remote, like having been born, and some present, like a supply of oxygen) that are necessary for the person's choosing as she does, or even sufficient, but that does not answer the question of *why* she chose as she did. It is something about our mental life, something about our preferences, that I propose as an ultimate explanation of free choice. This provides a sufficient condition for freedom of choice consistent with scientific determinism.

I want now to elaborate a sufficient condition of the power we exercise in freedom of choice presented earlier. The basis of my account offered earlier is preference. Recall that preference, unlike simple desire, is concerned with a profile of alternatives. In my first published paper on freedom of choice (Lehrer 1960), I noted that deliberation involves belief that you have alternatives. No alternatives to consider, nothing to deliberate about. I note here that preference, even if it does not involve deliberation, involves alternatives. Preference is preference over a profile of alternatives, at least the alternative of not choosing what you do. If you claim a person prefers an alternative, the natural question is "To what?" Preference is conceptually preference for one thing over another.

The claim concerning alternatives is important in contemporary discussion, provoked by the salient work of Harry Frankfurt (1969, 1971), of a person's doing what he desires. A person may do what he desires without reference to alternatives, especially if the desire is strong enough. We have all been there. We can lose our power of will, our freedom of choice, when desire rather than preference drives the engine of response. We have preference structures over profiles, sometimes profiles dominated by an alternative A that is the focus of the profile leading to the choice of A. The profile of preferences may explain the choice of A. However, it may fail to explain the choice. The choice may be the result of obsession or manipulation or coercion or just overwhelming desire. More subtle cases arise when the preference structure itself is manipulated. I may be persuaded to prefer an alternative when it is the power of persuasion of the other that explains my choice. The persuasion of leaders of cults sometimes shapes the preferences of followers in such a way that it is the power of the persuasive leader that explains the choice, for example, of suicide or killing another. It is the persuasive force of the leader that explains the choice rather than the preference. In short, preference, even over a profile of alternatives, can be manipulated.

Power Preference

I introduced the notion of a power preference, a higher-order preference for a preference structure, as a step in dealing with such problems. But higher-order preferences or even power preferences, though they support the idea that a person does what she prefers to do because she prefers to have that preference, do not fully deal with the problem. A power preference is a preference for the preferences in the preference structure concerning a choice of A. It is a preference in the preference structure since it concerns A and, therefore, is a preference for itself. But the question arises of why a person has the power preference for her preferred structure concerning an alternative A. If the explanation is manipulation, the power preference fails to ensure she has freedom of choice, that it is up to her how she chooses. The formulation of the problem contains the solution.

The problem, exhibited in a multiplicity of examples, is that some manipulation, coercion, or obsession explains the choice, perhaps by *causing and explaining* the power preference. What is needed to ensure that a power preference is the primary explanation is that the power preference is adequate to explain the choice without the need to appeal to anything else to supplement that explanation of the choice. Something may explain the power preference, but that is not needed to supplement the explanation of the choice by the power preference. The power preference must stand alone independent of other explanations as the *ultimate explanation* of the choice, that is, of why the person chose as she did. The power preference over the preference structure is included in the preference structure, as we noted. It explains the preferences in the structure's being a preference for them and, therefore, being a preference for itself; it is self-explanatory. The power preference may be explained by something else, but it stands alone, explained by itself, even if no other explanation is available. For economy of expression, I have referred to a power preference that is the ultimate explanation of choice as an *ultimate preference*.

Here is a more exact account of primary explanation:

PE. The power preference of a person for a choice is the *primary* explanation of the choice, an *ultimate preference*, if and only if it is minimally adequate to explain the choice without appeal to any supplementation of it.

That means ultimate preference is adequate to explain why the person chose as she did by itself independent of elaboration that might be added as supplementation. There is no need to appeal to any other different alternative explanation, including any explanation of the power preference itself.

This condition is intended to have the following critical consequence:

> PEC. If the power preference of a choice is the primary explanation of a choice, an ultimate preference, then nothing that explains the power preference is a primary explanation of the choice.

If what explains the power preference also explains the choice, then the power preference is not the primary explanation of the choice. So, if my power preference is manipulated by another to make me choose an action A, then my power preference is not the *primary* explanation of my choice, for it is the act of manipulation of the other that makes me choose A *albeit* by making me prefer to choose A.

Freedom of Choice Is Consistent with Determinism

We need some further premises to complete the defense of the consistency claim. The first of these premises is the sufficiency of the ultimate preference for freedom of choice. Here is my basic defense of the consistency claim. If choosing from ultimate preference is consistent with determinism and choosing from ultimate preference entails freedom of choice, then freedom of choice is consistent with determinism. Here is some elaboration.

> FWS. If the power preference of S for choosing A is the primary explanation of S's choosing A, that is, the ultimate preference for S's choosing A, then S exercises freedom of choice in A.

An additional premise is

ET. Explanation is not a universally transitive relation.

If explanation were universally transitive, then ipso facto anything that explained the power preference would explain the choice.

The examples of intransitivity are robust. Here is one. I am driving to keep an appointment with you at 7:00 p.m. at my favorite restaurant, Le Crocodile in Vancouver. On the way, I run over a nail and get a flat in the front left tire. I then change the tire and arrive on time at Le Crocodile. My running over a nail and getting a flat tire explains why I change the front left tire. My changing the front left tire explains why I arrive at Le Crocodile on time. But running over a nail and getting a flat tire do not explain why I arrive at Le Crocodile on time. The inference from A explains B and B explains C to A explains C I call the *transitivity fallacy*. Once we note that it is a fallacy, we can understand why conditions that manipulate my preferences to explain why I choose A preclude the preferences from being the primary explanation of the choice. It is the exercise of manipulation that explains my choice. My preference is, therefore, not an ultimate explanation. When the power preference explains my choice without being the result of manipulation, coercion, or obsession, to mention only a few conditions that might interfere with freedom of choice, the power preference explains my choice without the need to appeal to other conditions.

The transitivity fallacy concerning explanation is important for the defense of the consistency claim. The reason is that nomological deduction from antecedent events and laws resulting from determinism is universally transitive. So explanation of an event, including choice, must be distinguished from nomological deduction of the event from antecedent events and laws. I shall hereafter describe events that are the consequence of such deduction as being nomologically determined, or more simply as determined.

Determination without Explanation

Are all nomologically determined events explained by being so determined? As noted above, Sylvain Bromberger (1965), in reply to Carl Hempel (1962), showed that nomological deduction of an event from laws and conditions does not entail explanation. Thus,

NE. Nomological deduction of E from laws of nature L and conditions C does not entail that this deduction explains E in terms of L and C.

Bromberger's example was the application of the Pythagorean theorem construed as an empirical hypothesis about spatial relations. If you deduce the length of a distance between two objects triangulating a right triangle from some arbitrary object with a known distance from each of the two objects using the Pythagorean theorem, you will not, in spite of nomological deduction, have explained why the two objects are that distance from each other. An example may make this clear. I saw a rabbit lying on a grassy area not far from a coyote. They could see each other but neither moved. Given that coyotes hunt rabbits, I wondered why they were that distance from each other. Suppose you tell me it is easy to explain. You put a stick in the ground that forms a right triangle with the rabbit and the coyote and inform me that they're being the distance they are from each other is explained by measuring the distance from the stick to each animal and deducing the distance between them using the theorem. That would give you the correct distance by deduction but would not explain why the animals are that distance from each other. Deduction is not sufficient for explanation.

Once we take explanation as central to understanding freedom of choice, we obtain an understanding of the special role of preference, of a power preference, in explaining freedom of choice. The power preference is an ultimate preference that stands alone in the explanation of the choice. That makes the choice one of freedom of choice of the agent. We also understand why the counterexamples to freedom of choice work, and, at the same time, why nomological deduction of choice does not destroy freedom. The explanation of choice by preference must be primary for choice to entail that the choice is one of freedom of choice. Counterexamples explain the choice in terms of some factor other than preference of the agent, manipulation, compulsion, and so forth. Nomological deduction, useful for scientific inference, does not explain the choice. A primary explanation of choice by a power preference, the power preference as ultimate preference, blocks the counterexamples.

I conclude the discussion of the disconnection between nomological deduction and explanation with a caveat about science and explanation. The fact that nomological deduction embedded in scientific determinism fails to explain everything that is so deduced, as the example of the Pythagorean theorem illustrates, does not entail that anything must remain unexplained by science. Indeed, the failure of nomological deduction to explain does not entail that anything must escape the network of scientific explanation. It is consistent with the denial of nomological deduction to achieve explanation that, nevertheless, everything is in principle subject to explanation.

Maximizing Explanation without Determinism

I take it as a philosophical goal to maximize explanation, to explain as much as one can and leave as little unexplained as we must. But the failure of nomological deduction to explain everything does not entail that anything must remain unexplained. Consider an example from Wesley Salmon (1997) against the requirement that explanation require nomological deduction. At a certain point in the history of medical science, the fact that someone suffered paresis was explained by his having suffered syphilis; that is why he suffered paresis, which was a sound medical explanation, even though not everyone who contracted syphilis suffered paresis. Moreover, and close to the issue of freedom of choice, the existence of a power preference for choosing a given alternative may be the ultimate explanation for the choice, even though not everyone with a power preference for such a choice may make that choice. In some cases the power preference is the explanation, even the ultimate explanation for the choice yielding freedom of choice, while in others, when the power preference is manipulated by another, for example, the power preference would not be the ultimate explanation because of manipulation of it. Freedom of choice would be blocked.

Finally, once again, the failure of scientific determinism to maximize explanation does not abrogate the possibility of maximizing explanation. Scientific determinism is neither sufficient nor necessary for maximizing explanation. Maximizing explanation requires, as I (2007) have argued before, that the principle that completes maximizing explanation must explain itself as well as other things. The power preference that stands alone as self-explanatory in the explanation of the choice mirrors the first principle of explanation that stands alone as self-explanatory in the explanation of other matters.

Counterfactual Intervener and Power Preference

I conclude this part of the argument by noting that the appeal to a power preference as ultimate explanation to establish the consistency claim also contains a reply to Frankfurt's early (1971) argument, which he later amended (1988). The early argument was to the effect that an agent may act of his or her own free will though he or she could not have chosen otherwise than A. The example from Frankfurt (1971) was that of a counterfactual intervener able to ensure the agent's choice of A with the cognitive power to discern any sign that the agent would not choose to do A and rectify that by intervention. My reply is that the agent would be deceived about his or her freedom of choice. A power preference is a preference over the profiles of preferences containing the action A of choice. Those profiles contain alternatives to A as well as A, minimally the alternative of not doing A. If the power preference covers those profiles, then it contains other alternatives then A.

Now from the standpoint of the agent, whatever he or she chooses from the profile, including ones that involve choosing not to do A, will be considered by the agent to be his or her free choice, his or her ultimate preference. In examples where someone is empowered to intervene and manipulate the preferences of the agent, the agent is deceived about his or her free choice. The agent *thinks* that however he or she chooses, the power preference will be the ultimate preference. In classical examples of manipulation, the agent will be wrong because his or her choice will be explained by the exercise of manipulation.

In Frankfurt-style examples the agent will be deceived as well. The counterfactual intervener, though he does not intervene when the agent chooses A without intervention, would intervene if he knew the agent were to prefer not to choose A. He would manipulate the preferences of the agent so that the agent chooses A. The agent is mistaken in such examples in thinking that his power preference would be the primary explanation, the ultimate preference, of his choice no matter what he chooses. For if he were to choose other than A, the counterfactual intervener would have to change his plan to make the agent choose A, and it would be that *change of his plan* that must be included to explain the agent's choosing other than A. Thus, the power preference's being the ultimate preference for what the agent chooses from a preference profile entails that, whatever the agent chooses, he or she could have chosen otherwise. That is the power of the ultimate preference over a profile of preferences including alternatives other than what he chooses. The power preference as an ultimate preference of choice explains why the choice is free, a choice up to the agent.

Possible Worlds and Determinism

The account of determinism in terms of nomological deduction illustrates the role of determinism in science. However, philosophers often represent determinism in terms of possible worlds that track deductive relations. It has become popular to present determinism in terms of possible words for the simplicity of the formulation. Here is the simplest formulation. Determinism is true if and only if any possible world W, which has the same laws L as the actual world W_a and shares a complete state S_x of the actual world at a given time, is identical to W_a in terms of any complete state of S_y of W_p. This account of determinism assumes a temporal symmetry between past and future in terms of laws of nature. If one wanted an account that matched a temporally asymmetrical account, one might say instead that determinism is true if and only if for any possible world W_p which has the same laws L as W_a and shares a state S_x with the actual world W_a, then for any state S_y such that y is later than x, the possible world will contain S_y. More simply, given any state S_x of W_a that is also state of W_p, W_p will be identical with W_a at any time after the time of S_x. This view of determinism fits with idea of causality that the earlier states cause the later ones but not vice versa.

It is easy to extend the argument for the logical consistency claim of freedom of choice with a nomological deduction account of determinism to the possible worlds version. The extension of argument assumes that laws and, therefore, nomological relations are the same on both accounts. The consequence is that the possible worlds account like the nomological deduction version fails to yield an explanation of individual choices, or the states of the world containing them. Bromberger's argument is that nomological relations, whether or not they are expressed as premises in deduction, may fail to tell us why a person chooses as he does. Thus, even nomological relations that connect the past with the present by determining it may fail to explain why the present events occur. Once again, if explanation of why a person chooses as he does is what determines whether the choice was free, the logical consistency claim follows. It is logically consistent to acknowledge that past conditions determine present choices, as determinism tells us, and at the same time to affirm that it is a power preference, an ultimate preference, that explains the choice and, therefore, the freedom of it rather than the past conditions that determine it.

The issue of the logical consistency of freedom and determinism frequently rests on the account of asymmetric determinism according to which earlier conditions determine later conditions rather than the symmetric version of determinism with determining conditions running symmetrically in both directions. That is because it is determination or causation by earlier events of choice that is argued to create the logical inconsistency of determinism and freedom of choice. It is worth noting, however, that there is an oddity in the idea that the temporal order is what creates the logical inconsistency if the logical inconsistency is supposed to be the result of a connection, perhaps a modal connection, resulting from the law. One is reluctant to argue that the nomological connection of a future state of world limits our freedom in the present. I shall revisit this point later. I only notice the oddity of claiming that a nomological connection of a future condition being sufficient for a present choice is logically inconsistent with the freedom of the present choice or action. Our choices and actions that would be regarded as paradigms of free choice and action are often necessary conditions of future events, which entails that the future events are sufficient conditions of those choices and actions, whatever the past may have been like.

Determinism and Laws

The burden of this chapter is to consider the meaning of scientific determinism which rests, in turn, on the conception of scientific laws. There is something about laws that has motivated the arguments of logical inconsistency of freedom of choice and determinism, whether those of hard determinists or libertarians denying determinism. Even if antecedent determining conditions of choice expressing nomological relations do not explain choice, it remains open to the opponents of the consistency claim to argue that the nature of the laws supplying those relations has some feature that contradicts the consistency claim. To examine the case for laws contradicting the consistency claim, let us distinguish various conceptions of laws advanced by the opponents of the consistency claim. I begin with conceptions that make the logical\consistency claim easier to defend and progress to those that best support logical inconsistency.

Hume's Regularity Theory

Here are the standard accounts of laws starting with those that have the greatest appeal for defense of the logical consistency claim. First consider an account of laws as simple empirical regularities—all A are C. This is a view ascribed to Hume (1739), brilliantly explored by Helen Beebee and Alfred Mele (2002). Hume held that what we observed was not a necessary connection in nature but only a regular succession of events. However, he added that our impression of necessity was the habit of inferring the consequence C of the law from the occurrence of A. Some would formulate the view as simply a universal material conditional $(x)(Ax \supset Cx)$. That would not be accurate as an account of Hume. It would be anachronistic in a way that is contrary to Hume's meaning. The material implication sign has a modern technical meaning that does not do justice to Hume. You only need to note that if A were a contradiction, the material conditional would be true, but it would not represent the regular succession of observed events. For A would never be observed.

Moreover, there would be no habit of the mind to infer C from A. The point is that general description of the regularity must be understood as a claim about worldly occurrences rather than about an artificial logical function. So, the meaning of *All A are C*—intended to represent a succession of events—is not captured by the universal material conditional for Hume. Hume's intention is clear enough. When A is actually observed to occur, as it is, the occurrence of C is observed to follow. There is no modal connection observed. I note that for the universal state to be a law, another psychological condition was added by Hume, namely, a habit of the mind to infer C will occur when A does. He added that condition to account for our tendency to think of necessity associated with the regularity, though we have no impression of the necessity between events. That was important addition and a plausible psychological claim. I leave this as *Hume's regularity theory* of laws.

I maintain that the argument in defense of the consistency claim given for nomological deduction is sound for the regularity theory. The claim that a power preference is an ultimate explanation of a choice, one that is adequate to explain the choice without appeal to other conditions, is logically consistent with regularity. The reason is that regularity is often not explained. So that a condition regularly occurs with a choice does not entail that the condition explains the choice. Assuming the power preference does explain the choice, the power preference may be an ultimate explanation of the choice even if other conditions regularly occur when the choice does.

Scientific Laws: Universal Statements Warranting Subjunctive Inference

I shall take hereafter the general form of a law to be *All A are C*. Not all universal statements of this form are laws. Some are accidental and localized truths, like all the people now in this room have a philosophy degree. Other conditions must be added. Adding such conditions gives various accounts of laws beyond Hume's. One addition is that the universal statement must have the feature of warranting subjunctive inference to be a law. This was suggested at a conference at Brown University by Roderick M. Chisholm in 1959 without publication. I suggest that this addition, the subjunctive conditional addition, captures a role of such statements essential for scientific reasoning, as Chisholm proposed. So though it is controversial, I shall call this the *scientific conception of laws*.

The subjunctive formulation of the condition is *If A were to occur, then C would occur*. The contrapositive *inference—If C had not occurred, then A would not have occurred—*does not follow from the affirmative. That is, it is an invalid inference, as Pollock notes (1976). Another form of inference that is invalid for subjunctive inference, again as Pollock notes (1976), is *transitivity of* inference of the form *If A were the case, then B would be the case, and if B were the case, then C would be case, so if A would be the case, then C would be the case*. The example considered above of a person getting a flat tire applies to lack of transitivity of conditionals as well as to the lack of transitivity of explanation. The subjunctive conditional account of laws reminds one of Hume's suggestion of inference as habit of the mind, but it goes beyond an actual habit to the logic of subjunctive inference. An inference in terms of subjunctive conditionals is constrained by the formal features of such conditionals, such as failure of transitivity.

It is clear that this account of scientific laws does not undermine the argument given for the logical consistency claim. Given the failure of transitivity of subjunctive conditionals and the failure of the determining relation itself to entail explanation, it would be invalid to infer from determinism that there is a law for any choice C of an agent, such that there is some remote antecedent condition A, such that if A were to occur, then C would occur. To see this, note that all that follows from determinism is that if C occurs, then there is some antecedent condition B occurring before C that determines C, and also that there is some antecedent condition A occurring before B that determines B. But it does not follow that A determines C on the subjunctive account of laws; that is, it does not follow that if A were to occur, then C would occur. The transitivity of determining relations fails. Moreover, it does not yield a transitivity of explanation. Since a determining relation does not entail explanation, the fact that B determines C does not entail that even B explains C! So, the subjunctive character of the laws adds something to determinism beyond the regularity account, but nothing that could logically conflict with the ultimate explanation of the power preference for the choice C.

In an attempt to undermine the logical consistency claim, an opponent might add that there is always a law warranting subjunctive inference of the form *If A were to occur, then the agent would choose C*, and add that A is a temporally remote condition in the past beyond the control of agent. The defense of the consistency claim succeeds even against these additions, as I shall argue, but it must remain clear that these additions are not a consequence of determinism formulated in terms of laws as universal statements warranting subjunctive inference. This is a point about science and scientific procedure as well as a logical point. Scientific inference that allows one to conclude that a person will choose in a specific way does not depend in any way on a transitivity of subjunctive inference for the occurrence of the choice from remote events, the Big Bang, for example.

I turn, however, to the question of whether the truth of a universal statement, which warrants subjunctive inference whose antecedent is beyond the control of the agent, would rule out freedom of choice C as defined above, even if that is not entailed by scientific determinism alone. Is the presence of such a condition A, supposing A exists, an explanation of why the person chooses C that is required for the explanation of the person choosing C? Does the existence of A supplant explanation by the power preference of the person for choosing C? Surely not. The condition A might allow a person informed that A to infer that C without providing any explanation of why C exists. Once again, as we argued following Bromberger, not all sound inference, including subjunctive inference, is explanatory. The inference of C from A might leave us without any explanation of why C occurs in the same way that geometrical calculation of the distance of the rabbit from the coyote does not explain why the rabbit is that distance from the coyote. Inference, even subjunctive inference, of a choice does not entail an explanation of why the person chose as he did. The subjunctive warrant concerning possible cases beyond observed regularity is essential to the conception of a scientific law. Once again, the subjunctive character of the laws adds something to determinism, but nothing that could logically conflict with the sufficiency of ultimate explanation of the power preference in freedom of choice. The sufficiency of the ultimate preference entails freedom of choice and, at the same time, is logically consistent with determinism formulated in terms of scientific laws that warrant subjunctive inference. Thus, the logical consistency of freedom of choice and determinism under such laws is sustained.

Rejection of Hume's Theory

The sustenance of that logical consistency is important because Hume's regularity theory of scientific laws is defective for the reasons given above. It fails to distinguish nomological regularity from accidental regularity and fails to account for subjunctive and counterfactual inference. Though it would support the consistency claim if it provided a correct account of scientific laws, it fails to provide a correct account. I reject Hume's theory. The regularity theory is not a component of my defense of the consistency claim.

The preceding argument concludes my defense of the consistency claim. Scientific determinism in terms of scientific laws is consistent with freedom of choice because that freedom is adequately explained by human preference without appeal to other conditions. However, the history of the discussion of free will and determinism has included conceptions of laws governing events that fall under them so that the events are necessitated (most recently, Maloney 2023). This special doctrine of determinism becomes the doctrine of necessity. My interest in the consistency thesis is an interest in the unification of science with a conception of freedom of choice. However, others have conceived of laws of science that include attributes that preclude freedom of choice. Though I disagree with the attribution of these conceptions of laws to science, for I consider them metaphysical misconceptions, they must be discussed to avoid the charge of begging an important issue. I turn now to forms of laws that appear to lead to inconsistency with freedom of choice.

Modal Interpretation of Laws.

On classical accounts of freedom, when a person chooses C, then he could, under the same conditions, have chosen B instead of C. If those conditions include a condition A, and it is a law that all A are C, then the person could have chosen something instead of C even given the condition A and the law. The question that arises for a consistency theorist is how it is logically possible that the person could, under the occurrence of A, have chosen some alternative that excludes C given the law that all A are C. The answer depends on the relation or lack of relation between the modal notion of necessity in the law and the claim that the person could have not done C. It is impossible in standard modal logic that the following are all true:

(1) Necessarily, all A are C.
(2) A.
(3) Not-C.

But it does not follow that not-C by itself is *impossible* or that C by itself is *necessary*, given (1) and (2). All that is impossible is the conjunction of the three statements. In short, the modality cannot be detached. It may seem obvious that detachment of the modal operator is fallacious. A valid inference to the necessity of C requires the necessity of A as well as the necessity described in (1).

The modal theory by itself does not yield a popular alternative theory of determinism. I call it the *necessity theory*, which defines determinism as the doctrine that, given the laws of nature, everything that now occurs, or occurs at any other specific time, occurs necessarily. This conception of laws under the necessity theory is the basis for theories affirming that the laws of nature make things happen, that they govern how things occur. This doctrine is derived, in my opinion, from a theistic conception of a God laying down the laws of the universe. I bypass discussion of this ancient doctrine except to note that a modern version in which modal necessity replaces divine action depends on the doctrine of the necessity theory. This doctrine, if it is not to incorporate a modal fallacy, seems to depend on the assumption that past events are themselves necessary in the same sense as the laws, so that given the necessity of the events before the event considered, and given the laws of nature, the event is necessitated.

The argument:

(1) Necessarily, all A are C.
(2A) Necessarily A.
(3C) Not-C is impossible.

It is valid assuming the definition of *impossible X* as *necessarily not-X*. But now the inconsistency argument requires some argument that all past events that occur have the necessity of law, which is implausible, on one hand, as Joseph Keim Campbell (2007, 2011) argued, and, on the other hand, makes all appeal to laws appear irrelevant. That premise would be the doctrine of the metaphysical necessity of all that occurs, which is not a principle to which science is committed.

Some might be inclined to introduce a notion of conditional impossibility and conditional necessity to the effect that if (1) and (2), then C is conditionally necessary and not-C is conditionally impossible. This amounts to turning a modal fallacy into an account of necessity by redefining modal terms. Given this defined sense, there is no reason for concluding that a person cannot do what is conditionally impossible, odd as it sounds, for that amounts only to saying that the person cannot do what he does not do given the laws of nature. On such an account, if it is a law that all A are C, and S does C when A, then it is conditionally impossible S does not do A. But the conclusion that S had no alternative to doing C, that S could not have refrained from doing C, completely begs the question of consistency.

Since the laws on all accounts are universal statements, the doctrine of determinism may be formulated as the modal logic doctrine that any possible world that has the same laws as the actual world and shares a complete slice with the actual world will be identical to the actual world. It also allows for the forward-looking determinism doctrine that any world the shares a complete slice with actual world at a given time and has the same laws will be identical to the actual world at any subsequent time.

These modal views are distinct from empirical views that presuppose that a complete slice of the world is a slice that could be described completely in an observation language whose predicates are limited to distinctions that could be made by observation. Therefore, the formal necessity of pure mathematics cannot be transferred to the mathematical formulation of scientific laws based on observation. As Hempel (1958) noted in a central paper, observation is limited to differences that can be distinguished perceptually, but mathematical distinctions formulated in laws are not so limited. Consider the failure of transitivity of indiscernible observable differences. From the premise that there is no discernible difference between A and B and no discernible difference between B and C, it does not follow that there is no discernible difference between A and C.

This shows that indiscernibility cannot be equated with mathematical equality. The observation of measurements, even assisted by instruments, is limited to a least measure, implying the failure of transitivity of observation measurement. We are constrained at the level of observation language description to the conclusion that no matter how universal and exact the laws, prediction in terms of laws formulated in terms of observation predicates from one description of what we can observe in the world at a time, no matter how complete, will leave open the possibility that another world described in the same way at the same time and having the same laws might not satisfy the same description as the actual world at some later time. This is because of failures of transitivity resulting from the inexactness of observation predicates in comparison to mathematical ones. More than one exact mathematical description of the world at a time will correspond to an observation language description of the world at a time. Simply put, there are more different mathematical descriptions of the world than there are observation descriptions of what can be perceived at a slice of the world at a time.

Pereboom on Moral Skepticism

Having noted the failure of transitivity of indiscernibly observable differences, it is useful to here note the related failure of transitivity of indiscernible conceptual differences. The failure of transitivity of indiscernibility plays into the failure of transitivity of explanation in the defense of moral skepticism, most brilliantly articulated by Pereboom (2014). He begins with a condition of manipulation and argues ingeniously that there is no discernible difference between the case of manipulation and a sequence of conditions culminating in physical determinism of preference. I shall not consider the details. Though such arguments are ingenious and persuasive, they commit the transitivity fallacy of indiscernible difference. The limits of human discernment, like the limits of observation generally, exhibit failure of transitivity of difference. There may be differences a philosopher does not discern between A and B and B and C and C and D when there is an obvious difference between A and D. Given that difference between A and D, it is obvious from the difference why A provides a primary explanation, an ultimate explanation, for a preference that D does not.

We understand why manipulation is an ultimate explanation of preference, when we are in the dark as to why some physical state explains preference. For example, we would lack a sufficient explanation of why I preferred to write this very sentence at this very moment if we were just convinced some physical condition determined my preference just because physical determinism is true. For we would not know why I preferred what I did. Given our physical determinism conviction, whatever I preferred, or failed to prefer, we would be convinced it would be determined by some physical condition. But why would I prefer what I did rather than not? Whatever happened would be physically determined. Physical determinism leaves our why-question unanswered. The failure of transitivity of discernible difference yields the failure of transitivity of explanation. The conclusion, insisted on by Quine (1978), is that if a slice of a world is described in empirical terms, there will be multiple theoretical descriptions of that slice. So if possible worlds correspond or presuppose theoretical description of the world, there will be more theoretically distinguishable worlds than empirically distinguishable ones.

If the distinction between empirical description and theoretical discourse seems beside the point of consistency, just note that the claim that whether *All A is C* is law when C is a choice depends empirically on how people choose given A. It is not the case, to the contrary, that how they choose depends on whether *All A is C* is a law. The notion of dependence can be formulated in terms of subjunctive conditionals. X depends on Y if and only if X would not be the case if Y had not been the case. So *All A is C* would not have been a law if choice C had not occurred under condition A. But we cannot conclude that dependence goes in the other direction. It would be false to say that choice C would not have occurred under condition A, if *All A is C* had not been a law. The reason is that choice C might have occurred under other conditions even if *All A is C* had not been a law. Consider the example. I might have chosen to write this essay because there were conditions determining my writing it, my desires and beliefs about the results of writing it, for example, but it would be false to conclude that I would not have written the essay if those conditions had not been determining, in the sense of nomological sufficiency, of a law *All A is C*. Other conditions might have been determining, pleasing a colleague, for example, or it might have occurred without any antecedent conditions being determining, only antecedent conditions that would make it probable, Prob (A/C). Without any determining condition in terms of a law such as *All A is C*, I might have written the essay to please a colleague who wanted to include it in a collection she was editing, or there might have been a different law—*All B is C*. Different laws might have determined the choice. Different possible worlds have different possible laws.

Moreover, different empirical conditions might be determining under the same theoretical principles. I would argue, as I have with John Canfield (Canfield and Lehrer 1961), that the attempt to formulate universal scientific laws will confront the problem of including all boundary conditions in the universal principle to insulate it from empirical disconfirmation. That insulation will prove untenable given an unlimited number of needed boundary conditions. The consequence is that the assumption of complete generality of a law amounts to the assumption that further specification of boundary conditions does not matter. This is similar to the claim explained by Jenann Ismael (2016) that inference may be based on a universal statement treated as though it is concerned with a closed system, in my terminology, as though further boundary conditions are precluded or closed out from consideration. My proposal is that further boundary condition specification might defeat the inference. Think about a choice of career, to study law at Harvard, for example. There may be a set of antecedent conditions A when the choice C is made such that from A and L one could deduce that everyone in A would choose C, to study law at Harvard. But any attempt to formulate the condition A would leave open the possibility of some defeating condition D, maybe concerning a commitment to a beloved one to be in Germany, such that given A and D, C does not occur, and the inference is defeated. If the universal statement is used under consideration of defeasibility, that is functionally equivalent to treating the inference as stochastic or indeterminate in some form.

Laws Precluding Choice

I now turn to opposing accounts of laws and arguments. Carl Ginet (1966) and Peter Van Inwagen (1983) have argued most formidably against the consistency claim in terms of a different conception of laws of nature that preclude freedom of choice. Ginet's principal premise is that if *All A is C* is a law of nature, then when A occurs no one has any choice about whether C occurs. No one has any choice about whether the connection between antecedents and consequents of laws hold. Laws are beyond the control of human choice. Van Inwagen (1983) puts the point by saying that if the general principle *All A are C* is a law, then no one can render it false, which, like Ginet, means that if C is a human choice, then no one can render it false by her choice. Some scientific laws, those of astronomy, might convince us of the plausibility of this condition. However, if there are scientific laws about human choice, and if those laws are not reducible to other laws, the laws of physics, for example, the account becomes less plausible. Suppose C is a choice and consider the subjunctive conditional constraint on laws. Whether it is law that if A were to occur, then C would occur depends on whether people would choose C when A occurred. We will return to this later. But if you think that laws depend on how people choose, as I do, rather than choice depending on laws, that will be a reason for rejecting the idea that no one ever has any choice about C occurring when A occurs given that it is a law that all A are C. So my reply to Ginet is that he might advocate, as a metaphysician of genius, that determinism should be defined in terms of general principles whose truth does not depend on human choice. However ingenious the definition, it is not a definition of a scientific conception of laws when those laws concern human choice and depend for their truth on how people choose.

Van Inwagen, though not explicitly defining laws as universal statements whose truth does not depend on human choice, argues, with formidable genius, that determinism in terms of laws rules out human choice. He denies freedom of choice when that entails that the person could have chosen another alternative. Van Inwagen argues, in what is named his *consequence argument*, that if determinism is true, then the belief that people have alternative options in choice must be false. His argument has taken many forms, but the basic form of the argument is straightforward. If a person S who chooses C could have chosen B logically excluding C instead of C, then S could have rendered false the conjunction of laws L and any set of antecedent conditions D_C true prior to t at t' that in conjunction with L logically entails that S chooses C at t. Van Inwagen concludes no one can at t render false any statement that is either a law L or describes an antecedent condition D_C true prior to t at t'. Van Inwagen is assuming, moreover, the transitivity of the determining relation in such a way that t' might be some earlier time over which S had no control, perhaps not yet being born then. The conjunction of a statement of D_C at an earlier time t' together with the law L entails S chooses C at t. The conjunction of a statement of

D_C at such an earlier time t′ with a statement of L is a conjunction that S could not render false, because S could not render either the statement of D_C at t′ or the statement of L false. Van Inwagen (1983) concludes that S could not have chosen other than C at t because he could not at t render the conjunction false.

There are a number of objections to the argument. First of all, there is the simple objection that it does not follow from the fact that one cannot render false any specific conjunct of a conjunction that one cannot render the conjunction false. Take a simple example. There might two people X and Y each of whom will starve unless one is fed by a donation. So consider the conjunction X will starve and Y will starve. Now suppose they are in a distant land where the use of any donation is controlled by a third party who places conditions on donations. One condition is that, though a donation may be sufficient to save one person, if the donor specifies the exact recipient of the donation, then the donation will be rejected. By making a donation adequate to save one person, I can render false the conjunction X will starve and Y will starve. But I cannot render either specific conjunct false. I cannot render false the specific statement X will starve nor the specific statement Y will starve.

Moreover, as McKenna (2020) has explained, and as I (1980) previously argued in reply to Van Inwagen, elaborated forcefully by Lewis (1981), that even if it were conceded to Van Inwagen that no one could have chosen in a way that would have rendered something not a law, the consequence argument still fails. It requires, given the concession, that if a person could not have rendered a statement false that is a law, then, if the person could have chosen otherwise, the person could have rendered false the statement of the earlier condition about the past, which in conjunction with the statement of the law entails that the person chose what he did. But that does not follow. All that follows is that if the person had chosen otherwise, then the statement about the past *would have been* false. In short, if the person had chosen otherwise, as he could have, then either the statement of the law or the statement about the past would have been false. It does not follow that by choosing otherwise the person would have made either statement false. If he had chosen otherwise, then the conjunction would have been false, and at least one conjunct, therefore, would have been false. As an example, consider that if my parents had not conceived me, then I could not have chosen to write this essay. But it does not follow that there is anything I can do or choose to do that would render the statement false that my parents conceived me.

My most critical reply, however, is the one formulated against Ginet. The idea that scientific laws L have the property that no one could render them false is logically equivalent to the claim that no one could have chosen in such a way as to render any law L false. That, however, is logically equivalent to saying that S could not have chosen in such a way that what in truth is a law might not have been a law. The argument against this is the one given, namely, that laws depend on how we choose and not the other way around. If you think that laws are laid down in heaven by the Almighty to govern the universe, I can see how that might appeal to you. But that is theology, not science. Science tells us that whether something is a law about choice depends on how people choose. That is because a scientific formulation of a law about human choice is a general description of how people choose.

I reject the idea that acting contrary to what is a law would be a miracle, as Lewis (1981) suggested in reply to Van Inwagen. No miracle. Just a contingent fact about a contingent matter of what makes something a law about human choice, namely, how people in fact choose. If we hypothesize that some general principle is a scientific law about human choice and some choice fails to conform to the principle, the correct conclusion is not that the choice is a miracle but that the principle hypothesized to be a law fails to cover this instance. The scientific conclusion is that the general principle has been empirically disconfirmed and is not a universal scientific law. That is science instead of theology and perhaps traditional metaphysics. The arguments of Ginet and Van Inwagen are ones

I respect even as I reject the conception of laws assumed by them as failing to be scientific. I acknowledge they are arguments of genius, but as I have remarked following Reid commenting on the genius of Hume, it is sometimes genius and not the lack of it that leads to false philosophy.

Scientific Account of Laws: Inference and Explanation

I conclude with the appeal again to the account of scientific laws in terms of universal principles warranting subjunctive inference. That account supports the consistency claim known as *classical compatibilism*. Dependence cashed out in terms of subjunctive conditionals supports the view that whether something is a law about human choice depends on how we choose in the conditions of our human existence as opposed to the view that human choice is necessitated by laws of nature so that our choice depends on those laws. The laws, if scientific, depend on how we choose and how we would choose. That in turn depends on whether power preferences are ultimate explanations of choice, that is, ultimate preferences. That account allows for the possibility of subjunctive inference of all choice from antecedent conditions, and only imposes the constraint that some explanations, ultimate preferences, stand alone as adequate explanations of freedom of choice without supplementation. The consistency claim is supported by the consistency of affirming that not every inference in terms of laws is explanatory. The claim is further supported by noting that determinism formulated in terms of universal statements warranting subjunctive inference is consistent with the further claim that power preferences, though ultimate explanations, may themselves be explained. Explanation, as we noted, is not universally transitive. So even if every condition has an explanation, including power preferences, that is consistent with the claim that what explains the power preference for choice does not explain the choice.

Only the power preference, the ultimate preference, explains the choice, even though the power preference is itself explained. But explanation is not universally transitive. That failure of transitivity blocks the argument from the explanation of the choice in terms of explanatory ancestry. Explanation is not ancestral. Thus, power preference is an ultimate explanation of freedom of choice consistent with both scientific determinism in terms of scientific laws and with the broader claim that everything that occurs, even ultimate preference entailing freedom of choice, may admit of scientific explanation. A scientific explanation is an answer to the question, Why did that occur? But determinism alone does not entail all the answers. We consistently affirm that everything that occurs may be subjunctively inferred from laws and antecedent conditions, and, independently, that everything that occurs may be scientifically explained, though not by subjunctive inference from laws and antecedent conditions. Some explanations by power preferences are self-explanatory. They stand alone as adequate without need of supplementation by appeal to further conditions. Freedom of choice may be consistently unified with both scientific laws and complete explanation. The unification is a marriage of science and freedom of choice.

5
Freedom of Choice and Conflict Resolution

I began writing and thinking about free will motivated to consider the problem of free will and determinism. Since then, my interests have broadened into an investigation of freedom of choice in connection with causation, nomological relations, and explanation. That investigation led to the separation of the components. The logics of causation, nomological relations, and explanation differ. The most notable difference concerns the interaction between the notions. Nomological relations, which are universally transitive, do not entail causality or explanation. That is important. Some have argued that nomological relations alone rule out freedom of choice because of the transitivity of such relations connecting us with a past that is now beyond our control. I have argued that is a mistake. However, that leaves us with the possibility that all human actions are caused and admit of explanation. If that possibility is realized, does that eliminate freedom of choice? I conclude it does not, but that leaves some unanswered questions.

If actions are caused, how can they be free? If actions are explained, how can they be free? The answer given above to the latter question is that if a power preference is the ultimate explanation of the choice, then the preference will be a self-explanatory condition of choice that stands alone as an adequate explanation of the choice however much elaboration might be added. In short, whether the choice is free depends on how it is explained, not on whether it is explained. I would say the same of causality. A power preference may be the ultimate cause that stands alone as a cause of the choice. The power preference may be an adequate causal account however much might be added. That causal account is compatible with freedom of choice.

I have not pressed my argument in terms of causality because the use of the term "cause" has become connected with nomological relations and with explanation in a manner that tangles intuitions about causality with laws and hence nomological relations, on one hand, and explanation, on the other, dragging explanation into nomological relations that fail to sustain it. In short, it is assumed that causal relations logically track or are reducible to nomological relations, on one side, and that they track explanatory relations on the other. I would be inclined to think of causal relations naturally conceived as tracking explanatory relations. The explanatory relations manifested in causal relations are not universally transitive. So nomological relations are sufficient neither for explanation nor for causality. The same counterexamples used against the transitivity of explanatory relations are equally cogent against the transitivity of causal relations. To refer to the earlier example, my getting a flat tire on the way to dinner is not the cause of my arriving on time. My changing the tire is. That was caused by my getting a flat, but that is not the cause of arriving on time. Once again, explanation including causal explanation does not eliminate freedom of choice. Causal explanation may explain why my choice is free. Indeed, freedom of choice may incorporate causal explanation. In short, contrary to the libertarian, freedom of choice may be impossible without causality of a power preference. My choosing is free when I choose in accord with my power preference, and I have the power preference *because* I prefer to have that preference.

Reasoning and Preference

That said, I turn to some applications of the account of the theory of freedom of choice that puts the power preference on center stage in the explanation of freedom. One application is the social component in freedom of choice. The preferences of others as well as reasoning offered by others may influence choice. The problem is to distinguish when the influence of others can enlighten choice and the freedom of it as opposed to when it overcomes that freedom, leaving one in a kind of bondage to the others. Another component, which is an extension of the problem of the influence of others, is freedom of choice constrained by the general views as well as specific beliefs about the world that one chooses to accept. The two applications are both ones that involve transcendence from the first-order states, for example the desire to please others in social interactions, and the inclination to believe what we are told in accepting their view of the world. We transcend the first-order states to a higher order of rational preference of choice and acceptance of claims.

I discussed in an earlier chapter the influence of the preference of others on one's own that undermine freedom of choice. That occurs when the preferences of others are the primary explanation of the choice instead of the power preference of the subject. When the preferences of the other dominate our preferences, they disempower our active power, converting us into a passive subject. The subject is then passively acted upon rather than exerting an active power. The subject may be deceived into thinking that she is active, of course, but she is mistaken. When the subject has freedom of choice, the choice will be in response to a power preference that is an ultimate explanation and preference. However, we have noted that a person may respond to the preferences of another in a way that is compatible with freedom of choice. That results when the person prefers what the other prefers because he prefers to prefer what the other prefers. The distinction is subtle and requires amplification both for philosophical and for political purposes.

Whether the preferences of the other undermine freedom of choice, as opposed to allowing it, depends on the role of reasoning in preference. The reasoning of the other for her preference may become reasons of the agent himself. The question is when the reasoning of another person is compatible with the agent choosing according to a power preference of his own, an ultimate preference, as contrasted with the case in which the preference of the other dominates and binds the preferences of the agent, destroying freedom of choice. To clarify the distinction, we require some accounts of the formation of preferences that is so far missing from our account.

Weighted Preferences

The formation of preferences from lines of reasoning depends on the resolution of conflict between lines of reasoning in the individual. I am here advancing an ideally rational model for understanding conflict resolution as finding an equilibrium in the weights assigned from various perspectives within an individual that depends on the weight that he assigns to various lines of reasoning. The various lines of reasoning within an individual may be modeled as a variety of perspectives within the individual. A more controversial claim is that a useful way of viewing these perspectives is to idealize them as though they were perspectives of diverse individuals. This implies that the weight given to various perspectives within an individual to resolve conflict is an ideally rational model of the weights given to a variety of individuals. I have no proof that the best model for understanding ideal rational internal conflict resolution is the process of assigning weights to conflicting lines of reasoning of others to solve a problem of choice between the various lines of reasoning. I offer a model of external conflict resolution in equilibrium as an ideal theory of rational internal conflict resolution for whatever insight it provides.

The first observation I offer is that the assignment of weights to lines of reasoning of others is a higher level of response. Some might be inclined to think that assigning weights to reasonings of others, to return to our original example, Greta reasoning by appeal the record of scientific expertise, is simply a matter of how you *feel* about the reasoning of the others. One may have *feelings* about the way others reason, of course, that reflect associations and impressions. But assigning weights may involve rational judgment and comparison of alternatives subject to the reasoned evaluation of comparison. The judgment that being sober while driving rather than intoxicated should be given greater weight in evaluating whether to drive under the influence is a rational reflection of the higher-order system. It may oppose an inclination to drive and drink that may well be favored by a first-order desire and *feeling* that it is safe. When I discuss the assignment of weight to a line of reasoning, I am assuming that the line of reasoning is favored by a higher-order rational response.

Equilibrium and Fixed-Point Weights

Here is a formal model I have developed in detail with Carl Wagner (Lehrer and Wagner 1981). Suppose that a person has preferences from different perspectives:

$P_1, P_2 \ldots P_n$.

Suppose that I assign weights w_{ij} to the preference j from various perspectives i, which are

$wi_1, wi_2, \ldots wi_n$

such that all weights are in the interval 0 to 1 and sum to 1.

How do I find the weight w_j to assign to P_i that resolves my conflict between weights assigned to j from various perspectives i? Consider the weights w_{ij} assigned from different perspectives to P_j. Now suppose we find a set of weights (w_1, w_2 to w_n) to resolve the conflict between the weights assigned to w_{ij} from the various perspectives by multiplying the weights times the various w_{ij} that has the following structure:

$$w_1 w_{1j} + w_2 w_{2j} + \ldots w_n w_{nj} = w_j.$$

The conflict between various weights assigned to a preference at a given level is fixed by a set of weights in the sense that using that set of weights to find the weight to resolve the conflict is simply the weights in equilibrium that yield themselves back when used to average the weights assigned from the various perspectives to the weights assigned to a given preference. Weighted averaging is, I acknowledge, a theory of rational conflict resolution. The assumption is that if you give weights to conflicting alternatives, consistency requires that you modify your preferences by averaging in terms of the weights you assign. Otherwise, you are ignoring the weights you assign in forming a preference to resolve the conflict. Averaging has been defended by empirical study of Anderson (1968) and more recently Sivanathan and Kakkar (2017), and for the role of system 2, by Daniel Kahneman and Amos Tversky (1972, 1973, 2004).

I have argued in earlier chapters that a power preference among different preferences in a preference structure refers to itself as well as other preferences and is self-explanatory. If the preferences have their position in the preference ordering as a result of giving weights to the preferences from different perspectives, the weight given to the power preference is a fixed-point vector described mathematically in the earlier work with Carl Wagner (Lehrer and Wagner 1981). The fixed-point vector refers to itself in the sense that it resolves the conflict by remaining fixed in averaging the weights given to the weights given to a preference at a level. Being fixed here means that the weights in the fixed-point vector constitute a point of equilibrium. The weights of the power preference are unique in yielding themselves back in equilibrium as the weights to assign to the various perspectives. So, if the various perspectives give different weights to a preference, the conflict in weights will be resolved uniquely by a weight in a fixed-point vector. This means that the fixed-point vector finds a state of equilibrium in the assignment of weights to various perspectives, as proven of by Wagner in the appendix.

Consider an individual shifting perspectives from present pleasure to future health, and from both perspectives to living adventurously, as in the smoking case illustrated earlier. The person might assign different weights from one perspective to the other perspectives. Consider the conflict in the assignment of weights from different perspectives. The agent might assign less weight to the health perspective from the perspective of present pleasure. Then switching to the perspective of future health, he might assign less weight to the perspective of present pleasure. He might further assign more weight to the perspective of present pleasure than to the future health perspective from the perspective of living adventurously. He might also assign less weight to the living adventurous perspective from the perspective of future health. It is important to notice that the conflicting weights that a person assigns from one perspective to another may be considered as weights assigned from one perspective to the weights assigned to another perspective and vice versa. So, the weights assigned from various perspectives in the attempt to form preference for choice, though they reflect genuine and important aspects of reasoning and judgment, seem to increase conflict rather than to find a state of equilibrium that would resolve it.

However, the fixed-point vector resolves the conflict in terms of a set of weights that find an equilibrium set of weights to apply to the various perspectives. If the fixed-point vector is used to average the weights assigned from the various perspectives, it will always loop back on itself, yielding the same vector of weights, that is, the same weights to resolve the conflict. Thus, the fixed-point vector finds a point of equilibrium for the individual in assigning weights to the various perspectives, including, for example, perspectives of present pleasure, future health, and living adventurously in the smoking example. The conflicting preferences are given some weight, as the fixed-point vector assigns weights. The resolution of the conflict in terms of the fixed-point vector of weights provides a set of weights for averaging that is a point of equilibrium. It resolves conflict in terms of the weights assigned by the fixed-point vector. If you ask what weights to assign to the various conflicting weights assigned to reach equilibriums, the fixed-point vector provides the answer. If you ask what weights to assign to weights assigned in the fixed-point vector, the fixed point yields itself as an answer as the point of equilibrium. Like the power preference, the fixed-point vector yields itself back self-referentially as the rational weights of an individual. They are used to average assignment of weights from each perspective to obtain a power preference that explains and refers to itself.

Reasoning, Weights, and Preferences

How is weighted averaging in terms of a fixed-point vector connected with reasoning about preferences? Consider various preferences resulting from diverse reasonings I might have at the first level, P1. There are paths of reasonings $R_1, R_2 \ldots R_n$ that lead to a variety of preferences, $P1_1, P1_2 \ldots P1_n$. Consideration of these paths of reasonings is accompanied by a variety of factors, feelings, emotions, habits, and, not least of all, social and moral factors, that result in more weight given to some reasonings than others. The weights are not additional premises; a weight given to R_x is best interpreted as $w_i R_x$. An idea worth exploring is that the reason given the highest weight, $^{max} w_i R_x$, becomes $P1_x$. The question arises concerning the connection between the reasoning and the preference. Should we think of the preference conforming to the maximally weighted preference as a causal result of the reasoning? View the matter diachronically or dynamically as consideration of paths of reasoning leading to diverse preferences with the outcome that one is maximally weighted (hereafter described as the maximal reasoning) in the equilibrium of the fixed point resulting. It is natural to think of the preference as a distinct causal outcome of the reasoning. Suppose the maximal reasoning, though not identical with the preference outcome, combines with the preference at the same time in a fixed-point equilibrium. Then the process of forming a preference and reasoning about what to prefer may overlap. The preference may be the last line in the reasoning and a crucial constituent. Moreover, since the preference is a disposition to choose in the way preferred, given the choice and the absence of further consideration in a state of equilibrium, the reasoning may be part and parcel of what sustains the disposition.

If I consider why I choose in the preferred way, the reasoning may be indistinguishable from the preference as it sustains the disposition to choose. Of course, one may distinguish the preference from the reasoning in technical articulation of the preference. Though the description of the reasoning may be conceptually separated from the preference, the latter just is the disposition to choose in terms of the reasoning. This claim is not essential to my view of conflict resolution, and I acknowledge that the reasoning that leads to a preference in equilibrium, a disposition to choose in a given way, may be forgotten when the preference remains. So synchronically considered, it is the preference I have now in a point of equilibrium, and the preference may be considered as a state separated from the reasoning. Nevertheless, there are cases in which the forming of a preference causally amounts to giving weight to a path of reasoning in equilibrium.

Consider again the choice of whether to change jobs when you assess the advantages and disadvantages of each. The reasoning about which job to prefer, combined with the weight given to the reasoning, may become indistinguishable from the formation of the preference. At a certain point, a given line of reasoning receives more weight in the fixed point of equilibrium, and the preference is formed. Philosophers have talked about an act of will. But I propose that the act of will is the formation of preference. Some may object that you might fail to choose what you prefer. You might. They may describe that as weakness of will. But if failing to do what you prefer is weakness of will, then choosing from a power preference must be strength of will. I propose that there is no difference between choosing an act you prefer because you prefer to have that preference and the willing of the act. Put another way: philosophers are fond of using the expression, "It is up to me what I do" to express being in control. But if I choose to do what I prefer to do, and I have that preference because I prefer to have it in a state of equilibrium, then it is up to me what I then choose.

This argument reveals the importance of the power preference and the fixed-point vector of weights assigned to that preference in equilibrium. The fixed-point vector resolves conflict as explained above by aggregating the weights assigned from different perspectives in such a way that the vector remains fixed, yielding itself back in the process of aggregation. Averaging the weights assigned from various perspectives to a perspective in terms of fixed-point weights yields back the fixed-point weight assigned to the perspective in a loop. There is no remaining regress or instability of finding weights to resolve the conflict. The fixed-point finds a state of equilibrium in the assignment of weights. This equilibrium is the result of the way a person assigns weights; it is a summary of aggregation finding equilibrium rather than a foundation. The fixed point aggregates information a person has in a self-explanatory equilibrium rather than imposing an unexplained mathematical surd.

An illustration may be helpful. A reflective woman is trying to decide how to vote on Proposition 207 in an election in Arizona, the purpose of which is to legalize pot. One perspective is the perspective of respecting freedom of choice, call it F. Or consider another perspective from the standpoint her everyday aesthetics.

She dislikes the smell of pot, and it spoils her aesthetic experience. From that standpoint, call it A, she would be strongly opposed and would give the preference against 207 strong weight. However, she considers it also from the standpoint of the legal costs of illegality of pot, now in effect, which we could call the L perspective. The costs of illegality are profound in terms of the practical cost of enforcement and incarceration both for the law enforcement system and for the victims. From the L perspective she favors 207. From the L perspective, considering only costs, she favors 207. However, she forms another perspective of social concern, call this S, after consideration of statistics concerning the dangers of driving while under the influence of pot and social costs of accidents. Though she respects legalization, she still feels there should be restriction on the use of pot so that the use does not affect others in a negative and dangerous manner. Perspective F leads her to prefer voting for 207, as does perspective L, but perspectives A and S incline her to prefer voting against 207.

So how should she vote when she thinks about what perspective to take? A reflective stance combines various perspectives in deciding on problematic issues. What is notable is that to make a rational decision the person considering what she prefers with these conflicting preferences from different perspectives must combine, amalgamate, or aggregate how much weight to give to each perspective to find an equilibrium between perspectives. It will not do to simply count the perspectives. For the person may feel more strongly about the preferences from one perspective rather than from another. She may give more weight to one perspective, L, for example, than A, evaluating it as having more importance or value for outcome and how she votes. In fact, suppose the woman gives more weight to her preferences supporting F, giving more weight to the perspective of freedom of choice than to A or S, aesthetics or social costs. To form a preference, she must arrive at an equilibrium to amalgamate or more technically aggregate the weights of all four perspectives. How?

A brief analysis of the case shows the way in which reasoning about preferences can lead to a structure of preferences including a power preference over the preferences that resolves the conflict as it becomes a preference in the preference structure itself. The principle of aggregation depends on the assignment of weights. How much weight the person gives to preferences within a perspective gives us a vector of weights for each alternative under that perspective. But there is also the issue of weights given to the perspectives. The set of weights given to resolve conflict and find equilibrium corresponds to the power preference, and I will call it the power vector. How do we find the power vector? It is the fixed-point vector described above. This is the vector of weights used to average the weights assigned to the various weight vectors. The power vector remains fixed synchronically in the sense that it yields itself back mathematically in equilibrium at a given time. Thus, the fixed-point vector ends vacillation in weights that might be given to the weights assigned to various perspectives and finds equilibrium. I am not claiming, however, that the assignment of weights must be a conscious choice. The fixed point may be only a functional mode of response. It finds the power preference. The resulting power preference reveals itself in choice.

Trustworthiness and Rational Acceptance

I have spent many words over the relationship between ultimate preference and freedom of choice. Now I want to raise the question about the relationship between ultimate preference and rational acceptance. The first issue concerns the relationship between reasoning and preference. The second issue concerns the relationship between preference and rational acceptance. I want to present here the idea that evaluations of the trustworthiness of others play a major role in reasoning about preference as well as reasoning from preference to acceptance.

I began this work arguing that defensible freedom was my concern. Defensible reasoning obviously depends on reasoning to defend the preference, the power preference, and freedom of choice based on it. But reasoning may itself be defensible or indefensible. Consider then the case of reasoning, one's own or that of another. What makes the reasoning defensible? My proposal is that what makes the reasoning defensible is the trustworthiness of the evaluator of the reasoning. I initially put it in the first person for simplicity. Suppose I prefer a path of reasoning to others in favor of a course of action, whether smoking, how I vote, or what job I take. Am I reasonable in that preference? One might be inclined to reply that it depends on the character of the reasoning itself, that is, on the reasons and the inferential connection between those reasons. However, it is important to note I must accept the reasons and the inferences. That involves my preference for accepting those reasons and inferences rather than others. That will make the reasons and preferences my own, and if I am reasonable, the reasons and preferences that constitute the reasoning I accept will themselves be reasonable.

I could of course present further reasoning in defense of the reasoning I have already given and, moreover, present yet further reasonings in defense of my reasonings and so forth. The problem this raises is enmeshed in the complications of epistemology. That leads to a conclusion, suggested by Thomas Reid (1785), that I and my faculties must be trustworthy and not fallacious. My faculties by which I discern truth from error must not be fallacious as I accept my reasons. My reasoning, moreover, must be sound and distinguished from fallacious reasoning. In short, I must be trustworthy in what I accept and how I reason. Moreover, as I have argued elsewhere (Lehrer 1997a, 1997b), my being trustworthy will depend on what I prefer to accept and how I reason. But the reasonableness of the entire edifice of my preference, acceptance, and reasoning depends on a principle of trustworthiness, that I am trustworthy in how I proceed in these matters. Put very simply, if I am trustworthy in the pursuit of reason in what I prefer, accept, and how I reason, then I am reasonable in these, and if I am not trustworthy in the pursuit of reason, then I am not reasonable either.

Some caveats. Trustworthiness does not necessitate or require infallibility. We are fallible, as skeptics have taught us, but we can be fallible and yet succeed in achieving our goals. The most trustworthy guides to truth may fail us in special cases, but that does not keep us from obtaining truth and sound reasoning when truth and sound reasoning display themselves to us. But you may ask, what about the principle of trustworthiness itself? Is it reasonable to accept it? The answer is obvious. The principle of trustworthiness is something we accept, prefer to accept, and conclude from reasoning. It is like other things we accept, prefer to accept, and conclude from reasoning. If we are trustworthy in these undertakings in the pursuit of truth, then we are reasonable in accepting, preferring to accept, and concluding that we are trustworthy. To say this is simply to claim that the principle of trustworthiness in the pursuit of truth, when it is itself true and the conclusion of sound reasoning, yields itself as reasonable to accept, prefer to accept, and to conclude. There is an explanatory loop in the acceptance, preference for acceptance, and reasoning to the principle of trustworthiness. I have proposed that the principle of trustworthiness is a keystone in a circular arch supporting a dome together with the other states. If you conceive of the other states as constructing a dome of arches, then the principle of trustworthiness is a keystone loop circling around at the top to support all the arches. Of course, the keystone, as it supports the other stones in the arches, holding them in place, holds itself in place in the physical dynamics of mutual support. Some have written about a principle pulling itself up by its own bootstraps. That is an inferior metaphor because it is physically impossible. The keystone and the keystone loop are realized in actual physical structures such as arches in the sides of a chapel leaning against the keystone loop at the top.

With that bit of epistemology too quickly in place, I conclude that the reasonable acceptance of reasoning depends on the special epistemological trustworthiness of the subject. What about the reasoning of others? We have already noted that the freedom to choose to accept the preferences of others depends on an ultimate preference to prefer what the other prefers. That preference for the preference of the other must be a power preference for accepting the preference of the other, and it must be an ultimate preference when the choice to prefer exhibits freedom of choice. We also noted earlier (chapter 3) that a preference to follow a system of reasoning, a path of reasoning, which I called an *ultrapreference*, must itself be a power preference for following the path of reasoning. We now add that if the preference to be guided by a path of reasoning, whether internally invented or externally suggested by another, is reasonably preferred, then the individual must be trustworthy in what he prefers. We now add a condition unifying and connecting freedom and trustworthiness, namely this. To be trustworthy in what one accepts, prefers to accept, or how one reasons, one's preference for what one does must be an ultimate preference ensuring freedom of choice. Why? If you do not prefer these processes because you prefer to have that preference, that is, as an ultimate preference for proceeding in these ways, then you have no guarantee that the choice is your own or, in other words, that it was up to you what you accept, prefer to accept, or how you reason. In short, your preferences, if they are not ones you have because you prefer to have them as the primacy condition specifies, you may, rather than being a rational agent in the pursuit of reason, simply be a puppet in the control of another.

Rational Acceptance and Ultimate Preference

Many have held the view, to the contrary, notably Pereboom (2001), whom I discussed (Lehrer 2016), that a person may be a rational agent, reasonable in what she accepts, prefers, and how she reasons, simply because of the abstract form of the pattern of reasoning for what one accepts. I think that internet manipulators skilled at shaping forms of thought in unsuspecting passive receivers may already have undercut this agent-dismissed view of a rational agent or even a reasonable subject. My example (Lehrer 2016) was a pair of people, one ideally rational, call him Freerat, perhaps you wish to be the agent, who is a rational free agent, and the other is someone, Copyrat, whose brain processes are completely in the control of another, Control, who observes Freerat and installs the reasonings of Freerat in Copyrat, who has no control over his thought processes because Control completely controls those processes. My claim is that Copyrat is not a rational agent nor even a reasonable subject. The reasons in his thoughts are not his reasons and the reasonings are not his reasonings. He is a puppet. He is not a trustworthy person or agent in the pursuit of truth in what he accepts, prefers, or how he reasons.

The assumption that trustworthiness entails a power preference as an ultimate explanation of itself has deep consequences. The first consequence, and the most important, is that freedom of choice extends beyond freedom of conduct, often discussed under the topic of free will, to freedom of acceptance of our conception of the world. Reasonable and defensible freedom of conduct is an important but small sphere of reasonable and defensible freedom. In honesty, I am opening the door into Sartre's study. It was Sartre (1956, 1992) who argued that our freedom, embracing the totality of consciousness, extended to our freedom in what we accept as our worldview. In this context, he noted the meaning of his expression "Others are hell," which is as famous as it is misunderstood. Most philosophers grasp the meaning of Sartre's observation that our desire, he says passion, to make others accept our view of ourselves because we wish to control the freedom of others concerning what they accept about us involves a contradiction. It is their freedom we value and, at the same time, seek to control. That is the useless passion.

However, that hardly touches a basic issue of the other and myself in Sartre (1956, 1992), as I would now put it, that our being trustworthy in what we accept requires we acknowledge the same of the other. So, in our worldview, not just in our conduct, we must initially recognize that freedom of others and assume they are trustworthy in what they accept as we are in what we accept. Of course, we may come to reject what we initially recognize. This is most readily noticed in political or economic worldviews. Sartre broke with his best friend over the question of whether violence was acceptable to promote the communist revolution. And we do break all the time over political issues and religious issues. What I think is my contribution here is not that I note these differences—they are obvious. But it is less obvious that our reasonableness and freedom presupposes the initial recognition of theirs. I note that our initial recognition of the freedom and trustworthiness of others in what they accept is defeasible. Like us, they depend on fallible trustworthiness in what they accept.

My emphasis on the trustworthiness of others in what they accept is not intended to imply that we are in any way required to accept what they accept any more than we are required to choose what they choose. My point is different. Others are a potential source of reasonable acceptance when, and only when, we evaluate their reasonableness in a reasonable way. More deeply, whether they are a trustworthy guide to what we can reasonably choose and accept depends on our own capacity to evaluate their trustworthiness. This becomes problematic, however, when we recognize that our trustworthiness in evaluating others may depend on our evaluation of their evaluation of us. There is, therefore, a social loop of evaluation from our evaluation of them and their evaluation of us.

So how do I get the discussion of trustworthiness properly connected with power preferences and ultimate preference? The trustworthiness of others assumes that their trustworthiness depends on their ultimate preference. To be a rational, trustworthy agent depend on the power preference of the person as ultimate. So, my evaluations of others must be ones that I prefer to have because of my freedom, that is, my power preference as ultimate preference for those evaluations. Now the question is how the preferences of the others for what they accept and prefer, which reflects their trustworthiness in what they prefer, is connected with my own in a way that retains the ultimate explanation in terms of my preference. Their power preference when ultimate explains their preference and reflects their trustworthiness. But my evaluation of their preferences and their evaluation of my preferences can be a further source for me of my trustworthiness. How? My evaluations of others and their evaluations of others can be aggregated by a fixed-point vector aggregating the weights that we assign to each other in our evaluations of each other.

Consensus, Ultimate Preference, and Fixed-Point Vector

In the earlier work with Wagner (Lehrer and Wagner 1981) we considered the results of individuals in a group assigning weights to the probabilities of others and aggregating, that is, at an initial stage averaging, the probabilities of members of the group, including their own in the aggregation, to arrive at a new second-stage aggregated probability. From that stage, a new stage 3 would result from aggregation of the assignments at the second stage. The process may proceed from stage to stage, and a connection represented by positive weights may drive the process to consensus. We show that the consensus, when achieved as a limit of aggregation, amounts to arriving at a fixed-point vector for aggregating probabilities.

I repeat the formal model for resolving conflict among a group of individuals I employed for aggregating weights assigned to perspectives of a person:

$wi_1, wi_2, \ldots wi_n$

such that all weights are in the interval 0 to 1 and sum to 1.

How do I find the weight w_j to assign to P_i that resolves my conflict between weights assigned to i from various personal perspectives of i? Consider the weights w_{ij} assigned from different personal perspectives to P_j. Now suppose we find a set of weights (w_1, w_2 to w_n) to resolve the conflict between the weights assigned to w_{ij} from the various perspectives that has the following structure:

$$w_1 w_{1j} + w_2 w_{2j} + \ldots w_n w_{nj} = w_j.$$

The application of the personal model to resolving conflict among individuals in a group evaluating the trustworthiness of accepting some hypothesis or worldview requires only letting the subscripted weights apply to members of the group, 1, 2, and so forth, to n in the initial line: $wi_1, wi_2, \ldots wi_n$. After that modification of the model to include members of a group, the mathematics and application of the fixed-point vector is the same for evaluation of members of the group as for evaluations of perspectives within an individual.

In the present terminology, the weights individuals assign may be considered as comparative evaluations of the trustworthiness of assignment of reasonable acceptance of views of the members of the group. The mathematics of aggregation, including the constraints required for consensus, are complicated and will not be repeated here. But the idea applied here is that just as an individual may apply a fixed-point vector to represent the aggregation process of an individual applying a power preference to the diverse perspectives at various levels, so a fixed-point vector may be applied to represent the aggregation of the perspectives of various individuals. The weights assigned in either the individual case or the social case represent the evaluations of the trustworthiness of perspectives, whether of an individual or a group.

The fixed-point vectors in the personal or social case are used as an abstraction from the power preferences of individuals. We may view the social fixed point used to aggregate the evaluations of members of the group as standing in for a theoretical model of a power preference for the group. As such a model, it provides an ultimate explanation for the trustworthiness of the evaluations of the group and what it is reasonable to accept as trustworthy. The acceptance may be as general as a worldview or as specific as what you accept as the best outcome of a specific choice in an election.

Defensible Freedom and Social Trustworthiness

As I conclude this chapter, I find myself struck by the course of my journey in writing this book. I began with a notion of defensible freedom, thinking of it as ultimate preference incorporating an ultrapreference for a system of reasoning to defend the ultimate preference. The ultimate preference was a power preference that could stand alone as an explanation for freedom of choice. Now, at the end, I note that defensible preference rests on the trustworthiness of preference backed by the trustworthiness of acceptance and reasoning. In another formulation, defensible preference is a reasonable ultimate preference backed by reasonable acceptance and reasoning. However, in this chapter I have argued that the trustworthiness and reasonableness of preference depends on the evaluation of the trustworthiness of others and, finally, even on their evaluation of our trustworthiness. Reasonable self-trust and our being worthy of it depends on our evaluation of others and, indirectly, on their evaluation of us. The reasonable defense of preference ties us together with others.

If you ask what comes first in a process of forming a defensible preference, my answer defended earlier is that personal trustworthiness and interpersonal trustworthiness are tied together in a loop of mutual support and justification. The evidence for defense of preference is what you experience in the phenomenology of the feeling of successful support and justification. So just as the defense of ultimate preference considers the higher-order system of reason in my theory, or system 2 in Kahneman (2011), the defense takes us back to a first-order system of feeling and phenomenology that shows us what evidence and the success of reasonable preference is like. It is like the successful tying of an intricate macramé knot. The connection of the strands is complicated, but when the knot is properly tied and the strands beautifully support each other, you can see and feel that the knot is right. Even one naive about macramé and how to construct the knot can still experience the phenomenology of the well-constructed knot and how it all fits together. That is what the phenomenology of a defensible ultimate preference of freedom is like.

6
Freedom, Representation, and Consciousness

In the previous chapter, I noted that ultimate preference for accepting reasons and for accepting a worldview containing the reasons is an expression of freedom of choice. I do not mean to deny that there is a great deal of what we believe that is the result of biology, of how we are made, which may be the result of evolutionary processes that have proved effective in our survival. Much of what we believe is the result of automatic response, characteristically first-order representation, and is not the result of ultimate preference for choosing what we accept. In my terminology, belief is a first-order state, which is not something we freely choose, while acceptance, I have argued (Lehrer 1997b, 2000b, 2019), is a higher-order state, which is something we may freely choose. I do not think that first-order belief is always beyond alteration from what we ultimately prefer to accept in higher-order reflection. Admitting the possibility of penetration from higher-order acceptance into first-order belief, it is useful to contrast the first-order state of belief from acceptance. The latter, unlike the former, is within the power of freedom of choice and ultimate preference. The purpose of this chapter will take us closer to the views of Jean-Paul Sartre (1956) as we consider the role of consciousness and representation of conscious states in the ultimate preference for choosing a worldview. What is the role of consciousness in freedom of choice of our representation of our world and ourselves in our world?

A partial answer, advocated by many (Horgan and Tienson 2002; Kriegel 2009), is that consciousness supplies the phenomenology of our worldview. Does consciousness supply us with immediate awareness of what the experience is like and our conception of what our world is like? A computer would lack that awareness of what a world is like even as it might provide a complete description of the world. Here a puzzle presents itself. How can a complete description of what the world is like leave out or inevitably fail to fully represent what it is like? Frank Jackson (1982, 1986) was famous for his example of what I shall call Monochromatic Mary, or MM for short. MM has complete scientific knowledge of what color is like, but, being cursed with monochromatic experience, she does not know what the color red, or any other chromatic color, is like. The example produced a robust literature about whether MM can know what the colors are like if she cannot experience them. I agree that there is something that MM cannot know about the world she scientifically describes.

Consciousness and Acceptance

However, I want to introduce a person, Ralph, who is not color blind, who experiences colors, but still does not know that they are like. Ralph's problem is not a lack of conscious experience of color but an inability to represent what he experiences. You might be inclined to ask, What does Ralph need in order to be able to represent colors in addition to his conscious experience of them? The obvious answer is that he needs a capacity to convert consciousness into representation. Imagine that Ralph has suffered a brain injury that had the effect of rendering him unable to form representations of his experiences or anything else. I shall refer to Ralph as RR, representation-less Ralph. It is easy enough to imagine that RR has lost his ability to describe what he experiences because of a loss of descriptive abilities. But I am asking you to imagine a deeper loss of the power of representation so that he has lacks knowledge of what his experiences are like because he cannot represent them at all.

RR lacks representational knowledge of what colors are like, even though he has a conscious experience of the colors.

I have argued (2000, 2006, 2019) that representational knowledge, hereafter referred to simply as *knowledge*, depends on acceptance of representation. I now add that such acceptance depends on ultimate preference. Such knowledge demands our reasonableness in what we accept about the world. I concluded earlier that reasonableness depends on our evaluation of others, and, finally, even on their evaluation of us. You might ask, Is there any other ground for reasonable acceptance resulting from our freedom of choice in what we accept than the higher-order loop of our evaluating others and their evaluating us? Is there any exit from social trustworthiness to be found in individual freedom of choice? My answer is positive. It is to be found in the personal representations of consciousness. I acknowledge my indebtedness to both positivist and existential traditions in finding a ground for reasonable acceptance in the representations of consciousness that RR lacks.

RR illustrates that it is not consciousness alone that provides this ground for knowledge. It is our conception, or as I prefer, our representations of conscious experience, that grounds our knowledge of what it is like. Without representation there is nothing to accept. How we represent consciousness is often up to us. I argue against long traditions in empiricism that favor automatic or habitual responses of representation as the basis of knowledge. These deny our freedom of choice in the representation of consciousness. I argue that freedom of choice and, therefore, ultrapreference and the ultimate preference are involved in our reflective representations of consciousness. There is a form of representation of how we conceive of conscious experience that both has the plasticity of ultimate freedom of choice and, at the same time, provides the security of truth. Those representations become the materials of what we reflectively accept as the product of higher-order reflection.

Representation of Consciousness

I have recently discussed in detail the representation of consciousness and the relation of it to knowledge (Lehrer 2019). I did not emphasize the role of freedom of choice, though I have defended the thesis that the representation of consciousness employs a special higher-order process. I have called it *exemplar representation* and *reflexive representation* of the conscious state. I did not emphasize our freedom in exercising this process of exemplar representation or *exemplarizing* the conscious experience. Exemplarizing conscious experience is often fast, indeed, so fast that we are unaware of the process. A sharp pain is an example of a conscious state that is rapidly represented so that we know, almost immediately, what the state is like. It is interesting that under hypnosis in dental surgery, when you are told you will not feel pain, there is a sensation that at first may pass through the mind unnoticed, but it is then noticed as pain that, oddly, one does not mind. Aside from the question of whether the sensation is really pain, it is clear that before attending to it, perhaps distracted by the activity of the dentist, you have a sensation and lack a representation of it. This case is outside the experience of those who have not been hypnotized in this manner, however, so we turn to other examples.

Consciousness and Art

Consider a case that motivated my concern with exemplarizing conscious experience leading to reasonable acceptance. As a teacher of philosophy of art and also an artist, I was struck by the difficulty of getting students to attend to what a work of art is like and, crucially, to the potential of attending to their experience. In a case in point, where a student led me to attend to my own experience of an artwork, I was taking students to the Philadelphia Museum of Art, and we were looking at a Monet painting of a path

FREEDOM, REPRESENTATION, AND CONSCIOUSNESS 131

going off into the distance with a man on an ordinary pretty path, entitled *The Sheltered Path*. Figure 6.1 is a black-and-white image of the painting.

I wondered why the museum, which has so many brilliantly selected art objects, acquired this one. Nothing special. I could see the illusion of the path as a course of life, but that struck me as jejune. As I was about to turn my attention elsewhere, one student said, "The figure on the painting is coming toward us." Another replied, "No, he is walking way." Their disagreement got me to attend to my conscious experience of the painting. I realized I had not paid attention to what the figure of the man was like. Now I attended to the figure and what it was like. I realized there was a brilliance in painting the figure, impressionist style, with an ambiguity about

Figure 6.1 Claude Monet *Sheltered Path* (1873)
Philadelphia Museum of Art. Gift of Mr. and Mrs. Hughs Norment in honor of William H. Donner, 1972, 1972-227-1.

whether he was coming or going even though it was a realistic painting of a man moving on a path. My representation of the figure was the result of my attending to my conscious experience of it. My exercise of freedom of choice in directing my attention resulted in experiencing this figure as an exemplar of consciousness. I was now conscious of the special character of the figure. The ambiguity of the figure the two students noticed became part of my conscious experience. As a result of attending to the character of the figure in my experience, it became an exemplar representation of an ambiguous figure coming from the future into past and at the same time from past into the future on the path of life. My exemplar representation of my conscious experience, of what it was like, was a freely chosen act of attending to the conscious experience. I exemplarized it to know what my experience of it was like.

Reflexive Representation

Another example, suggested by the research of Adrienne Lehrer (Lehrer and Lehrer 1995) on discourse about the description of wine, is the sensation of taste in drinking beverages, specifically wine. Often you drink wine quickly, perhaps for the effect or to slack thirst, and you pay little attention to what the sensations of taste are like. In a wine-tasting course, or more casually a situation in which you are deciding what wines to purchase at a tasting, you may attend to the sensations of taste more carefully. The direction of attention to what the sensations are like may be enhanced if, following the instructions of Adrienne Lehrer in a wine description experiment, you consider whether certain verbal descriptors, "sweet," "sour cherry," "chocolaty," "cabernet," apply to a wine you are tasting. This directs your attention to sensations of taste. Even before responding to the verbal questions, you may pay special attention to your conscious experience. That direction of attention elicits conception and knowledge of what the conscious experience of the wine is like that was previously unnoticed, even if you have not considered how to describe the taste.

Once attention is focused, you have what I have called *reflexive representation* of what the taste is like even if you still lack verbal representation of it. For example, you may be uncertain whether to say it has a sour cherry taste. You first know what it is like in itself, apart from consideration of description based on similarity to anything else. Attention to the sensation produces a conception and knowledge of the sensation. The attention to the sensation produces a special form of conception or representation of what the conscious experience of it is like in itself. Attention gives birth to reflexive representation. How does attention to the sensation give rise to such representation, to an exercise of our capacity to know what the conscious experience is like in itself? The sensation itself becomes the reflexive term of representation of what the sensation is like. The sensation exhibits what it represents by representing itself. This is the process of exemplarization of the state of consciousness.

You do not need to get to an art gallery or drink wine for such an experience. If you are at a computer, direct your attention to the sensations in your fingers. Attending to the sensations, you come to know what those sensations are like even though they previously passed through your mind unnoticed as you were busy typing your message. Or take a John Cage moment. Close your eyes and direct your attention to your consciousness of what you hear. Having done that, turn from example to theory. As you attend to your conscious state, it becomes an exemplar, something like a sample of what you attend to. You convert your conscious experience into a symbol, an exemplar representation of what it is like in itself. You know what the auditory sensation is like because you have a reflexive representation of it. It represents what it is like by exhibiting itself as a representation of itself.

Theory of Reflexive Representation

Knowing what our conscious states are like requires our representation of them. Representation of our conscious states depends on attending to them. Attending to our conscious states can convert them into an exemplar for representation of themselves. That in brief is my theory of exemplar representation. Exemplar representation incorporates a process of reflexive representation. Reflexive representation takes the exemplar itself, a sensation for example, as the vehicle or term of representation. Reflexive representation of conscious states is special because it exhibits or shows you what it represents. The representation also shows us something about what truth is like beyond describing truth. It closes the gap between the representation and what it represents. The representation and the truth maker are one and the same. Exemplarizing the conscious state makes it a true representation of itself.

The term of reflexive representation, the sensation of look, the sensation of taste, the sensation of touch become representations of the sensations themselves. They are also extensively connected with other representations: representations of an artwork, representations of wine, and representations of keyboards. It is important to notice that the sequence of exemplar representation is not presented as a temporal sequence beginning with reflexive representation. Reflexive representation, of sensations for example, may arise at the same time as extended representation of other objects as a constituent of them. Such representations add to other representations, even those extending to the external world. Reflexive representations become constituents of other representations, sometimes of similar sensations and sometimes of external objects beyond sensations. They become part of the extended representations because they show us what our experience of those external things is like.

Reflexivity and Evidence

Reflexive representation of conscious experience gives those representations an empirical priority in the order of evidence. Reflexive representations become premises in reasoning to defend claims of the character and existence of external objects. That does not presuppose that reflexive exemplar representation temporally precedes our conception and thought about those objects. On the contrary, it may be necessary to block, or as Edmund Husserl (1989) suggests, bracket off, those thoughts, which already exist in order to engage in the sophisticated and often subsequent process of reflexive exemplarization used in defense of judgments about the world. The priority in the order of evidence and defense of a conception and judgment does not assume the temporal priority of acquisition. A scientist may conceive of a hypothesis before she acquires the sensory evidence needed to defend it.

To summarize, reflexive terms of representation may be extended and connected with representations of other conscious experiences and external objects. The connection of the reflexive representation with the representation of other things, which is a connection of meaning, shows us something about what those things are like and, therefore, becomes evidence to justify claims about the existence of those things. Our exemplar representation of external as well as internal objects shows us what they are like. This representation process also shows us what *we* are like as we represent, conceive, think, feel, and critically justify our knowledge claims with attention to the reflexive representation of what consciousness experience is like in itself. Finally, it shows us what our freedom of choice is like as we exercise that freedom when we attend to what the process is like.

Putting this discussion in the first person: I experience that it is up to me how I represent the world and myself, when I direct my attention to what it is like to exemplarize my experience. My freedom of exemplarization becomes salient in higher-order representations incorporating exemplars and my acceptance of them. Take the wine example. I attend to the taste in order to decide how to describe it. I may, if I am a philosopher of mind, note my freedom of choice in attending to the taste in this way. More plausibly, even if not a philosopher, I may note my freedom of choice in representing the taste as a sour cherry taste, as I note the option of representing it in other ways, for example, as a strawberry taste. The conscious direction of attention to the activity of representation and the acceptance of it exhibits to me my freedom of choice. Attention to higher-order representation and acceptance of reasoning shows us our further freedom of choice. Knowing, at a higher level, reveals the power preference of acceptance.

To press the theory further, the same is true of the connection between representation and states of the brain. The conscious states show us something about what the activity of the brain is like as we exemplarize those states. Exemplar representation becomes evidence of what the brain activity is like as we connect it with other representations of brain activity. We are not completely ignorant of what the brain is like before neurophysiology. Our exemplarization of consciousness gives us some pretheoretical knowledge of what the activity of the brain is like.

The point of these remarks is to exhibit that freedom of choice directs our attention to yield reflexive representation of our conscious experience. Moreover, freedom of choice connects reflexive representation beyond itself to our exemplar representations of the external world. Finally, the freedom of choice exercised in exemplar representation of our world loops back onto an exemplar representation of itself. Our direction of attention to exemplar representation takes us beyond first-order fast response to higher-order reflection. The connection between the thesis of freedom of choice and the exemplar representation of consciousness is a simple one. The need to defend what we think, how we conceive of our world, and even of our world in ourselves, directs attention from immediate needs to scientific, philosophical, and rational modes of thought. Our choices of what premises and reasoning to accept can take us from the first-level response to freedom of choice at the higher level. In the process, we experience the phenomenology of freedom of choice.

I have argued in previous chapters that the choice of what to do may be functionally equivalent to the acceptance of reasoning to choose that course of action. The acceptance of conclusions may, however, have a parallel role in thought not directed toward action. Preference and power preference may drive the engine of rational acceptance without being driven by the necessity of action. Moreover, our ultrapreference for a system of reasoning, elicited by abstract considerations of science or philosophy, may exhibit the freedom of choice supported by an ultimate power preference. Freedom of thought has the same structure as freedom of action. Ultimate freedom backed by ultimate preference for either a system of reasoning or the singular constituents of the system yields freedom choice. Sometimes such freedom is the result of attending to conscious experience. The attention is itself a matter of choice. When the choice is free it is sometimes defensible in terms of attention to sensory experience eliciting higher-order reflexive representation and knowledge of what the experience is like in itself. This mode of attention may evoke the need to block or bracket other forms of representation shaped by background information to obtain the purity of reflexive representation of the experience and what it is like in terms of itself. The reflexivity provides the truth security of using the experience to show us what the truth maker of the representation is like in a representational loop. Once the reflexive representation is connected to representations of other objects, the reflexive truth security is lost to gain information and explanation beyond reflexive representation. However, the reflexivity retains a role in evidence. The reflexive exemplar exhibits what it is like for us to experience other states and objects. It shows us what the represented things are like in our conscious experience of them.

Reflexive representation of conscious states has a deeper connection with freedom of choice than supplying us with truth secure representations to accept. As we confront our choice in how we connect reflexive representations with more general representations of the world, we appreciate the special role of reflexive representation in our freedom and plasticity of representation. To attend to what the conscious state is like in itself producing reflexive representation, we may block or bracket background representations to allow ourselves to pay attention to what the conscious state is like. That is a first exercise of freedom of choice in how we attend to what our conscious experience is like. It is a choice to exemplarize consciousness in a disconnected manner.

Ribosomes in the Surface of a Cell

The next exercise of freedom of choice is revealed as we connect the experience of exemplarizing our conscious experience yielding a reflexive representation to other representations, even theoretical descriptions of science. Take the example called to my attention by Otavio Bueno (2004, 2010) of the innovation that produced the electron microgram of the surface of a cell.

No one knew what the surface of a cell was like. When George Palade (1953, 1955), a distinguished scientist, looked at the microgram to produce his insight, he had to attend to his conscious experience of the microgram. I supply another image of ribosomes from a transmission electron microscope (the same instrument that Palade used) that may give you some indication what a conscious experience of them is like without any claim this is what Palade's experience was like (Figure 6.2).

Attention is the first exercise of freedom of choice. He knew what his experience was like even though he did not know how to interpret that initial reflexive representation of his sensory experience. It is essential to attend to what an experience is like in

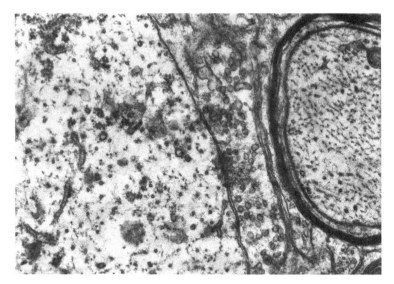

Figure 6.2 Transmission electron microscope (TEM) micrograph showing two synapses with clear synaptic vesicles.
Photo by Jose Luis Calvo, ©Shutterstock/537787369.

itself for controlled observation of the empirical data. That direction of attention was the first exercise of freedom of choice. The next exercise was the connection of the representation of the experience with background representations. That connection is the scientific interpretation of the initially bracketed empirical data of reflexive representation of experience. The acceptance of the thought that there are dots forming something like ribs in the electron microgram extends the reflexive representation of experience as evidence to justify a conclusion of the character of what is observed. The acceptance of that thought is an interpretation of the reflexive representation that exhibits freedom of choice. The next step, the insight of Palade, was the choice to extend the interpretation of the reflexive representation to the existence of RNA packets on the surface of the cell. That exercise of freedom of choice in scientific representation required experimental collaboration of the interpretation.

This story of science manifests how freedom of choice is exercised in our basic examples of the scientific construction of our world. That freedom is manifested in a defensible theory. The defense consists of an appeal to what the data is like in itself. That requires attention to what the experience is like, producing reflexive exemplarization of it. The direction of attention is exercise of freedom of choice. It may occur quickly, or as is often the case in scientific innovation, especially in the case of scientific revolution, it may require the discipline of bracketing or blocking a more standard interpretation to connect the reflexive representation of what the data in the experience is like in a new way, for example, in the experience of a microgram. The interpretation, as well as the acceptance of it, exhibits freedom of choice in the revolutionary case as well as in less striking instances.

My conclusion is that freedom of choice is exhibited in defensibility of a scientific claim involving direction of attention to sensory experience and the interpretation of it in data of representation of our world as well as in our acceptance of it. For our purposes, the most direct application may be the direction of attention to our experience of choosing and our acceptance of what such a claim is like. However, the aim of this chapter is to note the direction of attention toward sensory experience and toward the exemplarized content of conscious experience in what we generally accept about our world. Freedom of choice in world making, insisted on by Goodman (1968) and critically examined by Hilary Kornblith (2017), in the role of judgment, is not intended as an account of the origination of the reflexive representations. Nor is it account of how they originally extended to further representations of our world, though it may be suggestive. Freedom of choice becomes salient when we attempt to defend and justify those representations of our world, that is, when we reflect and defend what we think and do. The exercise of freedom of choice in representation and acceptance of views of our world is the manifestation of a higher-order form of thought and action, of attending to what we choose and to choosing itself. We and other creatures often think and act fast and without attention to our capacity for free choice and rational agency. The exercise of that capacity of ultimate freedom of choice requires the discipline to attend to it. It is worth the effort. You gain a world by freedom of choice.

Epilogue

Freedom and Two Systems

There is a question remaining after my theory of ultimate freedom is before us. What is the interaction between the first-order system and the higher-order system in our freedom? I have articulated a story, perhaps contrary to Kahneman, though indebted to his study, that the higher-order system is a source of freedom of choice and the leeway between options implied by it. My reason for the emphasis on the higher-order system of ultimate preference is that those, like Kahneman, who give emphasis to the role of the first-order system, system 1 in their theory, appear to ignore that they are writing from the viewpoint of system 2, the higher-order theory reflecting on how the systems function when they produce and articulate their theory. System 1, or the first-order system, may drive response in a useful manner, but obviously system 2, the higher-order system, forms preference and the ultimate freedom of choice that results. To come forth in all candor, the first-order system of desire and belief may have an important role in first-order functioning essential to survival, but it is not the hero of the story of agency. The higher-order system has the role of evaluating desire and belief, deciding whether desires should be satisfied and whether beliefs should be accepted. That system has access to the states of the first-order system and looping back onto itself to the states of itself. The evaluations of the higher-order system are a source of evidence, as I have argued (Lehrer 2011, 2019), as an evaluator of evidence of reflexive exemplarization. Evaluations and reasonings of the higher-order system form preferences, which are the ultimate explanations of choice in ultimate freedom.

Now the question arises as to the influence of the two systems on each other. My claim is that the first-order system may abrogate freedom of choice. It may cause responses to belief and desire that dominate higher-order evaluations, whether occurrent or implicit, that form preference. In short, sometimes the first-order system dominates response without the consideration of alternatives. Response without the actual presence of alternatives may occur, as our discussion of Frankfurt reveals. To avoid conflict that is verbal, I am willing to give up the expression of *free will*. A person whose actions are fully in accord with his desires and beliefs about how to satisfy them will certainly think that he is acting of his own free will. However, there is a kind of freedom that the person may be lacking, the freedom of choice, ultimate freedom. So, a person may act of his own free will but lack ultimate freedom. Putting this in the familiar expression, we can say that the person may enjoy a sense of free will, thinking, "I have done what I really wanted," while lacking ultimate freedom. The person is thinking in a moment of self-deception, "It is up to me what I do." Whether that person has ultimate freedom depends on what explains her response. Whether a person exercises freedom of choice depends on whether the preferences of the person, and especially the power preferences of the person, are a sufficient standalone explanation of choice.

Noting the role of explanation in determining whether a person has freedom of choice, the question is the connection between the free will of satisfying desires at the first order and freedom of choice exercised at a higher level. It all depends on what explains the response of the agent. Positive higher-order evaluation of desires and beliefs, especially concerning the necessities of life, may influence the formation of preferences to choose in a way that satisfies the desires and fulfills the needs. The evaluations of the desires and beliefs may contribute to the explanation of the preferences, including the ultimate preference that explains the choice. Preference, including power preference, even an ultimate preference, may be explained by desires and beliefs. The power preference may remain a sufficient explanation even though desires and beliefs explain the preference. That is fully compatible with freedom of choice explained by the ultimate preference. Remember that explanation is not transitive. The desires and beliefs that explain the formation of the ultimate preference, therefore, may not explain the choice. Preference is the ultimate explanation of the choice in freedom of choice.

Degrees of Freedom

It has been claimed that freedom admits of degrees (Corlett 2020). There are forms of freedom that do admit of degrees, as Corlett rightly claims, for example, the freedom to satisfy desires that admit of degrees. The free will to satisfy desires may also be constrained by internal and external factors that also admit of degrees. But can our account of ultimate freedom accommodate degrees of that freedom? Should it? There will be degrees of uncertainty, perhaps epistemic indeterminacy about explanation. That may lead one to erroneously mistake the degrees of uncertainty for degrees of freedom of choice. In many cases there will be uncertainty about the explanation. A person may *think* the choice was explained by the formation of preference when, in fact, higher-order evaluation would lack effective influence. It is like advice of another that has no influence, even though one's choice aligns with it. Should we say, therefore, that there are degrees of ultimate freedom of choice? It is clear that there are degrees of uncertainty about whether first-order states, desires, perhaps also fears and needs, explain a response or whether an ultimate preference of choice is the explanation. The first-order states may compel a response that undermines explanation in terms of a power preference. This generates degrees of uncertainty about whether a response is a free choice, but it does not entail that there are degrees of freedom. Most cases in which one talks about freedom of choice coming in degrees are deceptive misrepresentations of degrees of uncertainty about the explanation of the choice.

Are there, however, genuine cases of degrees of freedom of choice? There may be cases in which the uncertainty about what explains a response are also cases undermining the merit of an explanation. Suppose I live in an area where the danger of fire from climate change has created a deep fear of my house burning down. As a result of the fear, I may decide to insure my house when I encounter a manipulative insurance agent who enlivens those fears after gaining my confidence. I might buy insurance thinking it is a higher-order reflection on the dangers of fire and, therefore, think that I have exercised freedom of choice. I consider it reasonable to buy the insurance as I have evaluated the matter. But actually, I am frightened into buying it by the insurance agent. He scares many in the area to buy insurance, even though, in fact the risk of fire in the area is very low. In such cases, adequacy of the explanation of choice in terms of the power preference is undermined by the counterexplanation in terms of being manipulated by fear exploited by another. Must it be the case that one explanation is correct and the other incorrect? Must it be either first-level domination of fear or higher-order preference for the insuring that explains my response? Must the two factors be combined in an adequate explanation?

If the answer to the last question is affirmative, the power preference for the choice is *not* the ultimate explanation. The power preference does *not* stand alone as explanation for the choice. Ultimate freedom does not come in degrees. The example illustrates the salience of ultimate freedom in a satisfactory account of human agency. Whether a person is a full agent in freedom of choice depends on the standalone character of the power preference in the explanation of choice. Attention to higher-order evaluation in preference does not by itself ensure ultimate freedom of the agent. An agent, even one engaging in higher-order reflection, may be manipulated to respond to desires, fears, and needs at the first level supported by beliefs of the first level. These first-order states may explain those responses, rendering the higher-order reflections supererogatory or merely ancillary. Even if the power preference contributes to the explanation, that does not make it a standalone explanation for choice sufficient for ultimate freedom. Ultimate freedom does not come in degrees. It is ultimate.

The Return of Greta

I began this work by quoting Greta Thunberg: "How dare you!" The remark implied the power of freedom of choice on the part of the representatives of government in the climate change summit. Ultimate freedom explained by higher-order preference elaborates the power of freedom implied by her remark. What are the practical and moral implications of ultimate freedom? The most obvious is that representatives to the climate summit are morally obligated to consider the scientific information and statistical implications. That is right, but as Greta reads out the scientific information and statistical implications, we note our acceptance of their moral obligation to consider the information, to attend to a higher order, and, moreover, to attend to the reasoning to form preference and power preference for choice. If a higher-order power preference directs voting in a manner that expresses acceptance of the reasoning, then acceptance of the reasoning is a commitment to follow it. The critical point is that if representatives accept the reasoning, that is functionally equivalent to the formation of preference and power preference that is expressed in choice.

Some representatives may claim that they accept the reasoning Greta presents but express their freedom of choice to vote against the conclusions of the reasoning. The truth is the opposite. They hear the reasoning, but they do not accept it. Accepting the reasoning and preferring the conclusion it directs are connected functional states. The representatives who claim to accept the reasoning and vote to the contrary may choose of their own free will but fail to exercise ultimate freedom. They are choosing contrary to the reasoning of their system 2 in forming higher-order preference. My conclusion: the representatives rejected the reasoning presented by Greta, and she is confronting them with their moral obligation to accept the reasoning they are refusing to accept. You cannot have it both ways. You cannot accept a line of reasoning with a directive to form preference to choose and, at the same time, refuse to form that preference. Some people in positions of authority attend to the reasoning of system 2, the system of higher-order reflection of reason, and then turn away from the directive of the reasoning, refusing thereby to accept the reasoning. "How dare you!"

APPENDIX

On Keith Lehrer's Conception of a Power Preference

By Carl Wagner

This note is intended as an elaboration of Keith Lehrer's conception of your "power preference," over acts, as manifested in the fixed-point weight vector of a certain matrix of weights. The conflict between the values that you assign to an act from various perspectives, and its resolution, is modeled as follows:

1. You wish to determine a preferential ordering of acts $A_1,...,A_k$, each of which is available to you, where $k \geq 2$.
2. You intend to construct this ordering by introspecting about what real numbers $v_1,...,v_k$ best reflect the values that you assign to these acts, with preference among these acts reflected in the numerical ordering of these values.
3. Your dilemma is that the values you assign to these acts may differ, depending on which of the n perspectives $P_1,...,P_n$ you adopt. So you are faced with an $n \times k$ matrix $V = (v_{i,j})$, where $v_{i,j}$ is the value that you assign to act A_j from perspective P_i, where $1 \leq i \leq n$ and $1 \leq j \leq k$. Of course, if it should happen that, for each j, the numbers in the jth column of V are identical, so that

$$V = \begin{bmatrix} v_1 & v_2 & . & . & v_k \\ v_1 & v_2 & . & . & v_k \\ . & . & . & . & . \\ . & . & . & . & . \\ . & . & . & . & . \\ v_1 & v_2 & . & . & v_k \end{bmatrix}, \qquad (1)$$

your n perspectives are then in perfect accord regarding the values that they assign to each of the k possible acts, and immediately give rise to a preferential ordering of these acts.

In general, however, your value matrix V can be expected to take the form

$$V = \begin{bmatrix} v_{11} & v_{12} & \cdot & \cdot & v_{1k} \\ v_{21} & v_{22} & \cdot & \cdot & v_{2k} \\ \cdot & \cdot & \cdot & \cdot & \cdot \\ \cdot & \cdot & \cdot & \cdot & \cdot \\ \cdot & \cdot & \cdot & \cdot & \cdot \\ v_{n1} & v_{n2} & \cdot & \cdot & v_{nk} \end{bmatrix}. \qquad (2)$$

4. One way to resolve the discordant values in the above matrix would be to determine weights $w_1, w_2, ..., w_n$ to assign to the perspectives $P_1, P_2, ..., P_n$, and to use these weights to take a weighted average of each of the columns in V. . Many sorts of averages using many species of weights are possible here, but for simplicity let us assume that the weights are nonnegative and sum to 1, and that we employ weighted arithmetic (rather than, e.g., geometric, harmonic, or quasi-arithmetic) averaging. Then, the matrix product

$$[w_1, w_2, ..., w_n] \times V = [v_1, v_2, ..., v_k], \qquad (3)$$

where

$$v_j = w_1 v_{1j} + w_2 v_{2j} + \cdots + w_n v_{nj} \quad \text{for } j = 1, 2, ..., k, \qquad (4)$$

will integrate the values assigned to acts from various perspectives, with the numbers $v_1, v_2, ..., v_k$ defining a preferential ordering of the acts $A_1, A_2, ..., A_k$.

5. But how should you arrive at the weights $w_1, ..., w_n$? Lehrer imagines that you engage in an act of introspection that yields the $n \times n$ weight matrix

$$W = \begin{bmatrix} w_{11} & w_{12} & \cdot & \cdot & w_{1n} \\ w_{21} & w_{22} & \cdot & \cdot & w_{2n} \\ \cdot & \cdot & \cdot & \cdot & \cdot \\ \cdot & \cdot & \cdot & \cdot & \cdot \\ w_{n1} & w_{n2} & \cdot & \cdot & w_{nn} \end{bmatrix},$$

with nonnegative entries and each row summing to 1, and where w_{ij} denotes the weight assigned to perspective j from the standpoint of perspective i. It is natural to expect that the diagonal elements of W are the largest in their respective rows. But the remaining elements in those rows need not all take the value 0. Even from the perspective of sensual pleasure, for example, you might grant some weight to the perspective of ethics, or the enhancement of long-term physical or mental health. If all of the entries of W are positive, and in a variety of other circumstances (see Lehrer and Wagner 1981, Theorems 7.3 and 7.4), it does not seem unreasonable that there is implicit in W a unique row vector $[w_1, w_2, ..., w_n]$ that integrates the weights in W, with w_i denoting the weight of perspective P_i that emerges from W. Moreover, Lehrer claims, this row vector can be determined by finding the *fixed-point weight vector of W*, that is, by solving the system of linear equations

$$[w_1, w_2, ..., w_n] \times W = [w_1, w_2, ..., w_n], \tag{5}$$

subject to the conditions (i) $w_i \geq 0$, for $i = 1, ..., n$, and (ii) $w_1 + w_2 + \cdots + w_n = 1$.

But *why* should the weights w_i satisfy condition (5)? Because (and this is Lehrer's key insight) *the weights w_i given to various perspectives are appropriate for averaging **any** numerical assessments made from the standpoint of these perspectives.* In particular, it is appropriate that these weights be used to average the values assigned from various perspectives to various acts, as noted above in formula (3). *But it is also appropriate to use these weights to average the weights in the matrix W*. Suppose that the result of such averaging is given by

$$[w_1, w_2, ..., w_n] \times W = [w_1', w_2', ..., w_n']. \tag{6}$$

Then $[w_1', w_2', ..., w_n']$ is a competitor of $[w_1, w_2, ..., w_n]$ for use in formula (3). So in order for the enterprise of perspectival weighting to be coherent, it must be the case that $[w_1', w_2', ..., w_n'] = [w_1, w_2, ..., w_n]$, that is, that $[w_1, w_2, ..., w_n]$ is the fixed-point weight vector of W.

Bibliography

Anderson, Norman H. 1968. "A Simple Model for Information Integration." In *Theories of Cognitive Consistency: A Sourcebook*, edited by R. P. Abelson et al., 731–743. Chicago: Rand McNally.

Apaly, Nomy, and Schroeder, Timothy. 2015. "A Causal Theory for Acting for Reasons." *American Philosophical Quarterly* 52 (2): 103–114.

Balaguer, Mark. 2009. *Free Will as an Open Scientific Problem*. Cambridge, MA: MIT Press.

Beebee, Helen, and Mele, Alfred. 2009. "Humean Compatibilism." *Mind* 111: 201–223.

Bratman, Michael E. 1987. *Intention, Plans, and Practical Reason*. Cambridge, MA: Harvard University Press.

Bromberger, Sylvain. 1965. "An Approach to Explanation." In *Analytical Philosophy*, vol. 2, edited by Ronald J. Butler, 72–105. Oxford: Basil Blackwell.

Bromberger, Sylvain. 1993. *On What We Know We Don't Know: Explanation, Theory, Linguistics, and How Questions Shape Them*. Chicago: University of Chicago Press.

Bromberger, Sylvain. 2007. "Free Will and the Necessity of the Past." *Analysis* 67: 105–11.

Bromberger, Sylvain. 2011. *Free Will*. Key Concepts in Philosophy. Boston: Polity Press.

Bueno, Otavio. 2004. "The Drexler-Smalley Debate on Nanotechnology: Incommensurability at Work?" *International Journal for Philosophy of Chemistry* 10: 83–98.

Bueno, Otavio. 2010. "Models and Scientific Representations." In *New Waves in Philosophy of Science*, edited by P. D. Magnus and Jacob Busch, 94–111. Hampshire: Palgrave Macmillan.

Campbell, Joseph Keim. 2017. "P. F. Strawson's Free Will Naturalism." *International Journal for the Study of Skepticism* 7: 26–52.

Canfield, John, and Lehrer, Keith. 1961. "A Note on Prediction and Deduction." *Philosophy of Science* 28 (2): 204–208.

Cangelosi, Joshua. 2020. "Dual Freedom and the Power of Preference." Manuscript.

Chalmers, David. 1997. *The Conscious Mind*. New York: Oxford University Press.

Chisholm, Roderick M. 1966. "Freedom and Action." In *Freedom and Determinism*, edited by Keith Lehrer, 11–44. New York: Random House.
Churchland, Patricia. 1993. "Can Neurobiology Teach Us Anything about Consciousness?" *Proceedings of the APA*.
Cohen, Yishai. 2018. "Deliberating in the Presence of Manipulation." *Canadian Journal of Philosophy* 48 (1): 85–105.
Corlett, J. Angelo. 2020. "Free Will and Responsibility: To Tether or Not to Tether?" *Grazer Philosophische Studien* 97 (4): 559–574.
Darwall, Stephen. 2006. *The Second-Person Standpoint: Morality, Respect, Accountability*. Cambridge, MA: Harvard University Press.
Edwards, Paul. 1958. "Hard and Soft Determinism." In *Determinism and Freedom in the Age of Modern Science*, edited by Sidney Hook, 117–125. London: Collier Books.
Ehring, D. 1987. "Causal Relata." *Synthese* 73: 319–328.
Ferrier, James Frederick. 1866. *Lectures on Greek Philosophy and Other Philosophical Remains of James Frederick Ferrier*. Vol. 2. Edinburgh: W. Blackwood and Sons.
Fischer, John Martin. 1994. *The Metaphysics of Free Will: An Essay on Control*. Cambridge, MA: Blackwell.
Fodor, Jerry A. 1983. *The Modularity of Mind: An Essay in Faculty Psychology*. Cambridge, MA: MIT Press.
Frankfurt, Harry G. 1969. "Alternate Possibilities and Moral Responsibility." *Journal of Philosophy* 66: 829–839.
Frankfurt, Harry G. 1971. "Freedom of the Will and the Concept of a Person." *Journal of Philosophy* 68 (1): 5–20.
Frankfurt, Harry G. 1988. *The Importance of What We Care about*. Cambridge: Cambridge University Press.
Fürst, Martina. 2014. "A Dualist Version of Phenomenal Concepts." In *Contemporary Dualism: A Defense*, edited by Andrea Lavazza and Howard Robinson, 112–135. New York: Routledge.
Ginet, Carl. 1966. "Might We Have No Choice?" In *Freedom and Determinism*, edited by Keith Lehrer, 87–104. New York: Random House.
Ginet, Carl. 1996. "In Defense of the Principle of Alternative Possibilities: Why I Don't Find Frankfurt's Argument Convincing." *Philosophical Perspectives* 10: 403–417.
Goldsworthy, Andy. *Good images* on: *Google Images*. "Goldsworthy Striding Arches." 1980's.
Goodman, Nelson. 1968. *Languages of Art: An Approach to a Theory of Symbols*. Indianapolis: Bobbs-Merrill.
Goodman, Nelson. 1978. *Ways of Worldmaking*. Indianapolis: Hackett.
Hall, N. 2004. "Two Concepts of Causation." In *Causation and Counterfactuals*, edited by John Collins, Ned Hall, and L. A. Paul, 225–276. Cambridge, MA: MIT Press.

Hempel, Carl. 1958. "The Theoretician's Dilemma." In *Concepts, Theories, and the Mind-Body Problem*, edited by Herbert Feigl, Michael Scriven, and Grover Maxwell, 37–98. Minneapolis: University of Minnesota Press.
Hempel, Carl. 1962. "Deductive-Nomological vs. Statistical Explanation." In *Scientific Explanation, Space & Time*, edited by Herbert Feigl and Gordon Maxwell, 98–169. Minneapolis: University of Minnesota Press.
Horgan, T., and Tienson, J. 2002. "The Intentionality of Phenomenology and the Phenomenology of Intentionality." In *Philosophy of Mind: Classical and Contemporary Readings*, edited by D. J. Chalmers, 520–532. New York: Oxford University Press.
Hume, David. 1739. *A Treatise of Human Nature*. London: John Noon, bk. II, sec. III.
Husserl, Edmund. 1989. *Ideas Pertaining to a Pure Phenomenology and to a Phenomenological Philosophy. Second Book: Studies in the Phenomenology of Constitution*. Translated by R. Rojcewicz and A. Schuwer. Dordrecht: Kluwer.
Inwagen, Peter Van. 1983. *An Essay on Free Will*. Oxford: Clarendon Press.
Ismael, Jenann. 2007. *The Situated Self*. New York: Oxford University Press.
Ismael, Jenann. 2016. *How Physics Makes Us Free*. New York: Oxford University Press.
Jackson, Frank. 1982. "Epiphenomenal Qualia." *Philosophical Quarterly* 32: 127–136.
Jackson, Frank. 1986. "What Mary Didn't Know." *Journal of Philosophy* 83: 291–295.
Kahneman, Daniel. 2011. *Thinking Fast and Slow*. New York: Farrar, Straus and Giroux.
Kahneman, Daniel, and Tversky, Amos. 1972. "Subjective Probability: A Judgment of Representativeness." *Cognitive Psychology* 3: 430–454.
Kahneman, Daniel, and Tversky, Amos. 1973. "On the Psychology of Prediction." *Psychological Review* 80: 237–251.
Kahneman, Daniel, and Tversky, Amos. 2004. "Conflict Resolution: A Cognitive Perspective." In *Preference, Belief, and Similarity: Selected Writings by Amos Tversky*, edited by Eldar Shafir, 729–746. Cambridge, MA: MIT Press.
Kant, Immanuel. 1959. *Foundations of the Metaphysics of Morals*. Translated by Lewis White Beck. Indianapolis: Bobbs-Merrill.
Kapitan, Tomis. 1986. "Deliberation and the Presumption of Open Alternatives." *Philosophical Quarterly* 36 (143): 230–251.
Klein, Yves. IKB74 *Blue Monochrome*. https://www.sfmoma.org/artwork/99.372. 1956.
Kornblith, Hilary. 2017. "How Central Are Judgment and Agency to Epistemology?" *Philosophical Studies* 174: 2585–2597.
Kriegel, Uriah. 2009. *Subjective Consciousness: A Self-Representational Theory*. Oxford: Oxford University Press.

Kripke, Saul. 1975. "Outline of a Theory of Truth." *Journal of Philosophy* 72 (19): 690–716.
Lehrer, Adrienne, and Lehrer, Keith. 1995. "Fields, Networks and Vectors." In *Grammar and Meaning*, edited by F. R. Palmer, 26–48. Cambridge: Cambridge University Press.
Lehrer, Keith. 1960. "Can We Know That We Have Free Will by Introspection?" *Journal of Philosophy* 57 (5): 145–157.
Lehrer, Keith. 1961. "A Note on Prediction and Deduction," *Philosophy of Science* 28 (2): 204–208.
Lehrer, Keith. 1966a. "An Empirical Disproof of Determinism?" In *Freedom and Determinism*, edited by Keith Lehrer, 175–202. New York: Random House.
Lehrer, Keith, ed. 1966b. *Freedom and Determinism*. New York: Random House.
Lehrer, Keith. 1989. *Thomas Reid*. London: Routledge.
Lehrer, Keith. 1990a. *Metamind*. Oxford: Clarendon Press.
Lehrer, Keith. 1990b. "Preferences, Conditionals, and Freedom." In *Metamind*, edited by Keith Lehrer, 79–85. Oxford: Clarendon Press. chap. 3, reprinted from Peter Van Inwagen, ed., *Time and Cause: Essays Presented to Richard Taylor* (Dordrecht, The Netherlands: Reidel, 1980).
Lehrer, Keith. 1997a. "Freedom, Preference and Autonomy." *Journal of Ethics* 1: 3–25.
Lehrer, Keith. 1997b. *Self-Trust: A Study of Reason, Knowledge, and Freedom of Choice*. Oxford: Clarendon Press, 11–12.
Lehrer, Keith. 1998. "Reid, Hume and Common Sense." *Reid Studies* 21: 15–26.
Lehrer, Keith. 2000a. "Discursive Knowledge." *Philosophy and Phenomenological Research* 60 (3): 637–654.
Lehrer, Keith. 2000b. *Theory of Knowledge*. 2nd ed. Boulder, CO: Westview Press.
Lehrer, Keith. 2004a. "Freedom and the Power of Preference." In *Freedom and Determinism*, edited by J. K. Campbell, M. O'Rourke, and D. Shier, 47–69. Cambridge, MA: MIT Press.
Lehrer, Keith. 2004b. "Representation in Painting and Consciousness." *Philosophical Studies* 117 (1–2): 1–14.
Lehrer, Keith. 2006. "Consciousness, Representation and Knowledge." In *Self-Representational Approaches to Consciousness*, edited by U. Kriegel and K. Williford, 409–420. Cambridge, MA: MIT Press.
Lehrer, Keith. 2007. "Loop Theory: Knowledge, Art and Autonomy." *Proceedings and Addresses of the American Philosophical Association* 81 (2): 121–136.
Lehrer, Keith. 2011. "Evidentialism and the Paradox of Parity." In *Evidentialism and Its Discontents*, edited by Trent Dougherty, 55–68. New York: Oxford University Press, 2011.
Lehrer, Keith. 2012. *Art, Self and Knowledge*. New York: Oxford University Press.

Lehrer, Keith. 2014. "Thomas Reid on Truth, Evidence and First Principles." *Canadian Journal of Philosophy* 41, suppl.: 156–166.
Lehrer, Keith. 2016. "Freedom of Preference: A Defense of Compatibilism." *Journal of Ethics* 20: 35–46.
Lehrer, Keith. 2019. *Exemplars of Truth*. New York: Oxford University Press.
Lehrer, Keith, and Tolliver, Joseph. 2014. "Truth and Tropes." In *Mind, Values and Metaphysics: Papers Dedicated to Kevin Mulligan*, vol. 1, edited by Anne Reboul, 109–117. New York: Springer.
Lehrer, Keith and Wagner, Carl. 1981. *Rational Consensus in Science and Society: A Philosophical and Mathematical Study*. Dordrecht: Reidel.
Lewis, David. 1981. "Are We Free to Break the Laws?" *Theoria* 47: 113–121.
Luce, R. D., and Raiffa, H. 1957. *Games and Decisions*. New York: Wiley.
Lyons, Jack. 2009. *Perception and Basic Belief*. Oxford: Oxford University Press.
Maloney, J. Christopher. 2023. *Akratic Compatibilism and All Too Human Psychology: Almost Enough Is Free Will Enough*. Washington, DC: Lexington Press of Rowman and Littlefield.
McGee, Vann. 1991. Truth, *Vagueness, and Paradox*. Indianapolis: Hackett.
McGilchrist, Iain. 2009. *The Master and His Emissary: The Divided Brain and the Making of the Western World*. New Haven, CT: Yale University Press.
McKenna, Michael. 2012. *Conversation and Responsibility*. Oxford: Oxford University Press.
McKenna, Michael. 2020. "A Lost Lesson in Keith Lehrer's Reply to the Consequence Argument." *Grazer Philosophische Studien* 97 (4): 545–550.
Moore, G. E. 1912. *Ethics*. Oxford: Oxford University Press.
Naylor, Marjory. 1984. "Frankfurt on the Principle of Alternate Possibilities." *Philosophical Studies* 46: 249–258.
Nelkin, Dana L. 2004. "Deliberative Alternatives." *Philosophical Topics* 32: 215–240.
Palade, George E. 1953. "A Small Particulate Component of the Cytoplasm." *Journal of Applied Physics* 24: 1419.
Palade, George E. 1955. "A Small Particulate Component of the Cytoplasm." *Journal of Biophysical and Biochemical Cytology* 1 (1): 59–68. https://doi.org/10.1083/jcb.1.1.59.
Pereboom, Derk. 2001. *Living without Free Will*. Cambridge: Cambridge University Press.
Pereboom, Derk. 2014. *Free Will, Agency, and Meaning in Life*. Oxford: Oxford University Press.
Pollock, John L. 1976. *Subjunctive Reasoning*. New York: Springer.
Pollock, John L. 1986. *Contemporary Theories of Knowledge*. Lanham, MD: Rowman and Littlefield.
Quine, W. V. O. 1978. *The Web of Belief*. New York: McGraw-Hill.
Railton, Peter. 2014. "The Affective Dog and Its Rational Tale: Intuition and Attunement." *Ethics* 813–859.

Reid, Thomas. 1863. *The Philosophical Works of Thomas Reid, D. D.* Edited by William Hamilton. 6th ed. Edinburgh: James Thin.
Reid, Thomas. 1895. *Essays on the Active Powers of Man.* Edited by William Hamilton. 8th ed. Edinburgh: James Thin.
Robinson, Jennifer. 2020. KBPS, September 15. https://www.kpbs.org/news/2020/sep/15/nova-secret-mind-slime/.
Russell, Paul. 2004. "Responsibility and the Condition of Moral Sense." *Philosophical Topics* 32: 287–306.
Salmon, Wesley C. 1997. *Causality and Explanation.* New York: Oxford University Press.
Sartorio, Carolina. 2016. *Causation and Free Will.* Oxford: Oxford University Press.
Sartre, Jean-Paul. 1956. *Being and Nothingness.* Translated by Hazel E. Barnes. New York: Philosophical Library.
Sartre, Jean-Paul. 1992. *Notebooks for an Ethics.* Translated by David Pellauer. Chicago: University of Chicago Press.
Segerberg, Krister. 1983. "Could Have but Did Not." *Pacific Philosophical Quarterly* 64: 230–241.
Sivanathan, N., and Kakkar, H. 2017. "The Unintended Consequences of Argument Dilution in Direct-to-Consumer Drug Advertisements." *Nature: Human Behaviour* 1: 797–802. https://doi.org/10.1038/s41562-017-0223-1.
Smilansky, Saul. 2000. *Free Will and Illusion.* Oxford: Clarendon Press.
Sosa, Ernest. 1991. *Knowledge in Perspective: Selected Essays in Epistemology.* Cambridge: Cambridge University Press.
Strawson, Galen. 1994. "The Impossibility of Moral Responsibility." *Philosophical Studies* 75: 5–24.
Strawson, P. F. 1962. "Freedom and Resentment." *Proceedings of the British Academy* 48: 187–211.
Stalnaker, Robert. 1968. "A Theory of Conditionals." In *Studies in Logical Theory: Essays*, edited by Nicholas Rescher, 29–45. New York: Oxford University Press.
Taylor, Richard. 1966. *Action and Purpose.* Englewood Cliffs, NJ: Prentice-Hall.
Timpe, Kevin. 2012. *Free Will: Sourcehood and Its Alternatives.* 2nd ed. London: Continuum.
Velleman, J. David. 1992. "What Happens When Someone Acts?" *Mind* 101 (403): 461–481.
Vihvelin, Kadri. 2000. "Libertarian Compatibilisms." *Philosophical Perspectives: Action and Freedom* 14: 139–166.
Wallace, R. Jay. 1994. *Responsibility and the Moral Sentiments.* Cambridge, MA: Harvard University Press.
Watson, Gary. 1975. "Free Agency." *Journal of Philosophy* 72: 205–220.

Watson, Gary. 1987. "Responsibility and the Limits of Evil: Variations on a Strawsonian Theme." In *Responsibility, Character, and the Emotions: New Essays in Moral Psychology*, edited by Ferdinand Schoeman, 256–286. Cambridge: Cambridge University Press.

Widerker, David. 1995. "Libertarianism and Frankfurt's Attack on the Principle of Alternative Possibilities." *Philosophical Review* 104: 247–261.

Watson, Gary. 2004. *Agency and Answerability: Selected Essays*. Oxford: Oxford University Press.

Yeats, Jack. 1949. *The Gay Moon*. http://onlinecollection.nationalgallery.ie/view/objects/asitem/204/32/sortNumber-asc?t:state:flow=28ba903f-d7b9-4b6c-a610-ab732b37ed71.

Index

For the benefit of digital users, indexed terms that span two pages (e.g., 52–53) may, on occasion, appear on only one of those pages.

Figures are indicated by *f* following the page number

active power
    agency and, 22, 34–35, 57–58
    conflict resolution and, 108
    intention and, 53
    justification and, 15–16, 17–18
    power preference and, 19–20, 22, 32–33, 36–37, 39, 40, 42, 45–46
    reason and, 22, 57–61
    ultimate explanation and, 36–37, 40, 42
    ultimate preference and, 5
agency
    active power and, 22, 34–35, 57–58
    causality of, 64–66
    compatibilism and, 7–8
    overview of, 7–8
    power preference and, 26–27, 34–35, 64–66
    reason and, 11, 57–61, 64–66
    systems of thought and, 12, 140–41, 142–43
    ultimate freedom and, 11, 145–46
    unification of, 7–8
Anderson, Norman, 111
arationalism, 73–75
Arpaly, Nomy, 27–28
art, 65–66, 130–32, 133

Balaguer, Mark, 6
Beebee, Helen, 89–90
Bratman, Michael E., 53
Bromberger, Sylvain, 36–38, 78, 83, 87–88
Bueno, Otavio, 138

Campbell, Joseph Keim, 30–31, 95–96
Canfield, John, 99–100
causation. *See* agency; determinism
Chisholm, Roderick M., 57–58, 90–91
Churchland, Patricia, 13–14
Cohen, Yishai, 14
compatibilism
    agency and, 7–8
    classical compatibilism, 75, 76, 104–5
    determinism and, 6, 76, 104–5
    explanatory burden of traditional forms of, 75
    overview of, 6
    power preference and, 35–36
conflict resolution
    active power and, 108
    consensus and, 123–25
    defensible freedom and, 125–26
    equilibrium and, 110–13
    fixed-point weights and, 110–15, 123–25

conflict resolution (*cont.*)
  overview of, 106–10, 125–26
  power preference and, 66–67, 106–9, 111–12, 114–15, 117, 118, 120–21, 124–25
  reason and, 107–9, 113–20
  systems of thought and, 111
  trustworthiness and, 117–23, 124–26
  ultimate explanation and, 108, 121, 122–23, 125
  ultimate preference and, 117, 120–26
  ultrapreference and, 120
  weighted preferences and, 109–10, 111, 113–17
consciousness
  acceptance and, 128–29
  art and, 130–32, 133
  exemplar representation and, 130, 131–32, 133–37, 140, 142–43
  existential conception of, 33–35, 121, 127, 129
  knowledge and, 129
  manipulation and, 33–34
  overview of, 127–28
  phenomenology of world through, 127–28
  power preference and, 135–37
  reflexive representation and, 130, 132–41
  representation and, 128–30, 133, 136–37
  ribosomes in the surface of a cell and, 138–41, 139*f*
  ultimate freedom and, 29–30
  ultimate preference and, 127, 129, 137
consensus, 123–25
consistency claim. *See* compatibilism; determinism
Corlett, J., 144–45

could have chosen otherwise, 3–4, 5–6, 15, 25–26, 42–44, 78–79, 86
counterfactual intervener, 85–86

desire, 3, 39–42, 49–56, 79, 142–46
determinism
  compatibilism and, 6, 76, 104–5
  could have chosen otherwise and, 78–79
  counterfactual intervener and, 85–86
  definition of, 7
  explanation and, 78–79, 83–85, 87–88, 104–5
  freedom of choice as consistent with, 81–82
  Hume's regularity theory and, 89–90, 93–94
  inference and, 104–5
  laws precluding choice and, 100–4
  manipulation and, 97–98
  maximizing explanation without, 84–85
  modal interpretation of laws and, 94–97
  moral skepticism and, 97–100
  nomological deduction and, 78–79
  overview of, 6–8, 76–78, 104–5
  Pereboom on moral skepticism and, 97–100
  possible worlds and, 87–88
  power preference and, 7–8, 79–82, 83–88, 90, 91–93, 104–5
  reason and, 74–75
  rejecting Hume's theory and, 93–94
  scientific laws and, 76, 77–78, 88–89, 90–94, 99–101, 103, 104–5
  ultimate explanation and, 78, 80, 84–86, 90, 92–93, 97–98, 104–5
  ultimate freedom and, 17–20, 25–26

ultimate preference and, 76–77, 80–81, 83–84, 86, 87–88, 92–93, 104–5
universal statements warranting subjunctive inference and, 90–93
without explanation, 83–84

exemplar representation, 130, 131–32, 133–37, 140, 142–43
existential conception of consciousness, 33–35, 121, 127, 129
explanation. *See also* ultimate explanation
active power and, 40
determinism and, 78–79, 83–85, 87–88, 104–5
inference and, 104–5
maximizing of, 84–85
nomological connection and, 36–38
power preference and, 25–26, 33–36, 80
primary explanation, 80–81
reason and, 64–66

Fischer, John Martin, 47, 49–50, 71–72
Fodor, Jerry, 10–11
Frankfurt, Harry
conflict among preferences and, 22–23
could have chosen otherwise and, 39–42, 79, 85–86, 143
counterfactual intervener and, 41–42, 85–86
deliberation and, 15
desire and, 3, 39–42, 49–50, 79
free will defined by, 3
moral responsibility and, 3–4
power preference and, 39–42, 85–86

freedom, ultimate. *See* ultimate freedom
freedom of choice overview, 1–8
agency, 7–8
compatibilism, 6
could have chosen otherwise, 5–6
determinism, 6–8
freedom, 6–7
free will distinguished from freedom of choice, 3–5
leeway theory, 8
moral responsibility, 3–5
moral skepticism, 3–5
overview of, 1–5
philosophical method of current volume, 1–3
preference requirement, 3
sourcehood view, 8
ultimate explanation, 7–8
ultimate preference, 5, 7–8
unification of science, 7–8

Ginet, Carl, 15, 100–1, 103–4

Hempel, Carl, 36–37, 83, 96–97
Hume, David, 15–16, 47, 50–51, 76–77, 89–90, 93–94
Husserl, Edmund, 30–31, 135

intentionality, 31–32, 53
Ismael, Jenann, 99–100

Jabr, F., 30
Jackson, Frank, 127–28
justification, 3–4, 15–18, 20, 72, 125–26

Kahneman, Daniel, 9–10, 11, 111, 125–26, 142–43
Kakkar, H., 111
Kant, Immanuel, 47, 70–71
Kapitan, Tomis, 14
Kripke, Saul, 61–62

leeway theory of freedom, 8, 16–17, 29–30
Lehrer, Adrienne, 132–33
Lehrer, Keith, 3–4, 19f, 21–22, 24–26, 48–49, 56–57, 60, 84, 104–5, 117–19, 125, 128–29, 130, 133, 134–41, 149–51
Lewis, David, 102–4

manipulation, 33–34, 35, 38–42, 55, 57–58, 62–63, 79–80, 81, 82, 83–85, 86, 97–98
McGee, Vann, 61–62
McGilchrist, Iain, 10, 11
McKenna, Michael, 3–4, 30–31, 102–3
Mele, Alfred, 89–90
metamental ascent, 51–53
modal interpretation of laws, 94–97
Moore, G. E., 56
moral responsibility, 3–5
moral skepticism, 3–5, 97–100

Naylor, Marjory, 29–30
Nelkin, Dana, 14
nomological deduction, 36–38, 78–79

optionality, 9–10, 14, 15–16, 18–19, 30–31
overviews
  agency, 7–8
  compatibilism, 6
  conflict resolution, 106–10, 125–26
  consciousness, 127–28
  determinism, 6–8, 76–78, 104–5
  freedom of choice, 1–8
  power preference, 5–8, 149
  reason, 47–48, 68–71
  systems of thought, 9–11, 142–47
  ultimate explanation, 5, 7–8, 35–36
  ultimate freedom, 9–11, 29–31
  ultimate preference, 5, 7–8

Palade, George, 138–40
paradox of reason, 47–48, 62–63, 64–66, 67–69, 73
Pereboom, Derek, 3–4, 97–100, 120–21
Pollock, John, 16–17, 43–44, 91
possible worlds, 42–45, 87–88
power, active. *See* active power
power preference. *See also* ultimate explanation
  active power and, 19–20, 22, 32–33, 36–37, 39, 40, 42, 45–46
  agency and, 26–27, 34–35, 64–66
  compatibilism and, 35–36
  conflict among preferences and, 22–25
  conflict resolution and, 66–67, 106–9, 111–12, 114–15, 117, 118, 120–21, 124–25
  consciousness and, 135–37
  could have chosen otherwise and, 5–6, 42–43, 44–45
  definition of, 5, 24–25
  degrees of freedom and, 144–46
  desire and, 39–42
  determinism and, 7–8, 17–20, 79–81, 82, 83–88, 90, 91–93, 104–5
  explanation and, 25–26, 33–36, 80
  Frankfurt's example and, 39–42, 85–86
  internal structure of, 62–63
  manipulation and, 38–39, 62–63
  metamental ascent and, 51–53
  overview of, 5–8, 149
  possible worlds and, 44–45
  preference of others and, 66–67
  preferences over preferences and, 31–33
  reason and, 21–22, 26–28, 51–57, 59–60, 66–70, 72–73
  role in freedom of choice of, 33–35, 39, 59–60, 61–67, 73–75

as self-explanatory and self-referential, 33–34, 59–61, 65–66, 111
semantic structure of, 62–63
systems of thought and, 22, 125–26, 143–46
trustworthiness and, 121–23, 125
ultimate freedom and, 17–20, 21–22, 25–26, 31–33
ultimate preference's relation to, 5–6, 8, 24, 35–36, 38–39, 40–42, 63–64, 67, 70, 80, 83–84
ultrapreference and, 72
ungrounded preference and, 61–63
preference. *See* conflict resolution; power preference; ultimate preference

Quine, W. V. O., 98

Railton, Peter, 10
reason
 active power and, 22, 57–61
 agency and, 11, 57–61, 64–66
 arationalism and, 73–75
 choice and, 26–28
 conflict resolution and, 107–9, 113–20
 desire and, 49–56
 determinism and, 74–75
 explanation and, 64–66
 internal freedom of choice and, 49–51
 metamental ascent and, 51–53
 overview of, 47–48, 68–71, 73
 paradox of, 47–48, 62–63, 64–66, 67–69, 73
 power preference and, 21–22, 26–28, 51–57, 59–60, 66–70, 72–73
 preference of others and, 66–67
 primacy condition and, 63–64
 rational acceptance, 117–20, 137

solving paradox of, 67–68
 ultimate explanation and, 63–65, 67–70, 74–75
 ultimate freedom and, 11, 21–22
 ultimate preference and, 63–64, 68–69, 73, 120–23
 ultrapreference and, 71–72
 ungrounded preference and, 61–63, 68–69
reflexive representation, 130, 132–41
Reid, Thomas, 14–18, 32–33, 57–58, 103–4, 118–19
representation, 128–38
responsibility, moral, 3–5
Rothschild, Anna, 30

Sagan, Carl, 30
Salmon, Wesley, 84–85
Sartorio, Carolina, 29–30
Sartre, Jean-Paul, 33–34, 72, 121–22, 127
Schroeder, Timothy, 27–28
scientific laws, 36, 76, 77–78, 88–89, 90–94, 99–101, 103, 104–5
Segerberg, Krister, 56–57
Sheltered Path (Monet), 130–31, 131*f*
Sivanathan, N., 111
skepticism, 3–5, 15–16, 97–100
Sosa, Ernest, 2
Stalnaker, Robert, 43–44
Strawson, Peter, 3–4, 30–31
systems of thought
 agency and, 12, 140–41, 142–43
 belief and, 12–13, 18
 conflict resolution and, 111
 definition of, 9–10
 evaluation and, 18
 overview of, 9–11, 142–47
 power preference and, 22, 125–26, 143–46
 ultimate freedom and, 9–13, 29–31, 142–43, 146

Taylor, Richard, 57–58
thought systems. *See* systems of thought
Thunberg, Greta, 12, 33–34, 45–46, 146
Timpe, Kevin, 29–30
Tooliver, Joseph, 133
trustworthiness, 117–23, 124–26
Tversky, Amos, 11, 111
two systems of thought. *See* systems of thought

ultimate explanation. *See also* power preference
  active power and, 36–37, 40, 42
  conflict resolution and, 108, 121, 122–23, 125
  definition of, 5, 35
  determinism and, 78, 80, 84–86, 90, 92–93, 97–98, 104–5
  manipulation and, 38–39, 82, 98
  nomological connection and, 36–38
  overview of, 5, 7–8, 35–36
  possible worlds and, 44–45
  reason and, 63–65, 67–70, 74–75
  systems of thought and, 142–46
  ultimate preference and, 5, 7–8
ultimate freedom
  agency and, 11, 145–46
  conflict among preferences and, 22–25
  consciousness and, 29–30
  definition of, 9, 13–14
  determinism and, 17–20, 25–26
  evidence and, 20–21
  explanation and, 25–26
  justification and, 15–17
  as leeway theory of freedom, 29–30
  necessary and sufficient conditions for, 13–14, 26
  optionality and, 9, 14–15
  overview of, 9–11, 29–31

  power preference and, 17–20, 21–22, 25–26, 31–33
  practical and moral implications of, 146–47
  preferences over preferences and, 31–33
  reason and, 11, 21–22
  as source theory of freedom, 29–30
  systems of thought and, 9–13, 29–31, 142–43, 146
ultimate preference
  active power and, 5
  conflict resolution and, 117, 120–26
  consciousness and, 127, 129, 137
  could have chosen otherwise and, 5–6, 42–44
  definition of, 5
  determinism and, 76–77, 80–81, 83–84, 86, 87–88, 92–93, 104–5
  overview of, 5, 7–8
  possible worlds and, 44–45
  power preference's relation to, 5–6, 8, 24, 35–36, 38–39, 40–42, 63–64, 67, 70, 80, 83–84
  preferences of others and, 67
  primacy condition and, 63–65, 70, 71
  rational acceptance and, 117–23
  reason and, 63–64, 68–69, 73, 120–23
  systems of thought and, 142–45
  ultimate explanation and, 5, 7–8
ultrapreference, 71–72, 120, 125, 129, 137
ungrounded preference, 61–63, 68–69

Van Inwagen, Peter, 15, 56–57, 100–4
Velleman, J. David, 71–72
View of My Path, A (Lehrer), 18, 19*f*
Vihvelin, Kadri, 27–28

Wagner, Carl, 110, 111–12, 123
Watson, Gary, 30–31